GESTATIONAL SURROGACY

The Definitive Guide

VICTORIA FERRARA

*To my amazing and brilliant spouse, Michelle
and our wonderful sons, Sal and Nick*

Printed in the United States of America

First Printing, 2023

ISBN 979-8-218-24878-9

Worldwide Surrogacy Specialists, LLC
2150 Post Road
Fairfield, CT 06824

www.theferraralawgroup.com
www.worldwidesurrogacy.org

The information presented herein represents the view of this author as of the date of publication. This book is presented for informational and educational purposes only. Due to the rate at which conditions change, the author reserves the right to alter and update the information contained herein. While every attempt has been made to verify the information in this book, the author does not assume responsibility for errors, inaccuracies, or omissions.

Contents

Foreword

Navigating the steps of family building, particularly surrogacy, can be challenging, confusing and for some, even scary. That's why books like this, written from the inside and grounded in truth and transparency, are such an essential read for parents-to-be, their friends and families who support them, and the professionals with whom they collaborate.

Attorney Ferrara draws from her thirty-plus years of experience in the field and presents one of the most thorough yet understandable roadmaps to breaking down this multistep process into simple, manageable steps with an awareness of not only each critical component but also of how they fit together and how one affects the other.

I first met Vicki twenty-five years ago when we collaborated on one of her most personal and heartfelt creations: her own family building journey. As her fertility specialist, I had the privilege of partnering with her on what started simply as a successful course of treatment but soon became much more: two decades of professional collaboration with hundreds of clients seeking surrogacy-related services, not to mention a valued friendship.

I don't know of anyone who is more personally and professionally suited to write this book than Vicki. The ethics and values that she holds most dear—transparency, fairness, inclusiveness, and balanced regard for all parties involved (intended parents, donors, surrogates, and all the children born to the intended parents)—have led her to become one of the most trusted and admired surrogacy attorneys in the United States. She understands the complexities and vulnerabilities inherent in the process, and armed with her supreme legal knowledge and expertise, deftly balanced with a refreshing dose of practical common sense, she has been able to advocate for and protect those pillars of surrogacy treatments in the United States: uncompromising safety, expert counsel and guidance, and unwavering ethics.

As you read these pages, you will see Attorney Ferrara's constant reaffirmation that family building is a deeply personal process, and as such, it remains essential that providers at every level must do everything they can to ensure surrogacy journeys that are not only safe, ethical, and effective but also nontransactional and deeply human. These journeys don't just create babies; they create, connect, and ensure families that would otherwise never exist, and allow parents-to-be to approach their journeys in ways that feel uniquely right for them.

MICHAEL B. DOYLE, MD

Acknowledgments

There are so many teachers I have had along the way to making this book happen. With so many years as a lawyer practicing in the field of assisted reproductive technology law, I have had the privilege of working with many talented, smart, competent professionals including lawyers, physicians, mental health providers, nurses, and others. You know who you are. I have learned so much from all of you along the way, and I thank you for sharing with me your experience and humanity in doing this work of family formation.

I would like to thank my spouse, Dr. Michelle Loris, for always being my sounding board, for always encouraging me to keep writing, and for being the most loving and supportive spouse I could ever hope for.

I would also like to thank my good friend, Michael B. Doyle, MD, whom I have known since the inception of my work in surrogacy and who always encouraged me to develop and expand the work of my surrogacy agency, Worldwide Surrogacy Specialists, LLC.

I must acknowledge and thank the many intended parents and surrogates who I had the privilege and honor to counsel over the years. Through my ongoing work with them, I was able to share in the joy of the parents having their children, and the humanity of the amazing surrogates making their selfless gifts and contributions to helping these parents have children and build their families. My life's work with intended parents and surrogates formed what was the genesis for this book.

Also, my team at Worldwide Surrogacy Specialists shows me so much about how this work of helping people have children through surrogacy should be done. Specifically, I want to acknowledge and thank Kim Goodrich, Serena Lugo, Beth Anne Ferraro, Jennifer McArthur, Anna Mazza, Jackie Unger, Julie Veilleux, Lynden Scarano, Casey Oakley, Cara MacLean, Andrea Ambrose, and Maureen Hand, as well as Deb Smey, Melinda Lewis, and Sean Ryan. I also want to thank our former team member, Molly Corcoran, as she did some hands-on research and work on some of the parts of the book.

Lastly, I want to thank my mother for encouraging me to be a lawyer. I was not always thrilled with her motivations about what she wanted for me, but the truth is that because of becoming a lawyer, I was able to find my way into this amazing work of sharing people's most profound human journeys.

Introduction

In 2012, I wrote and published the book, *Gestational Surrogacy: A Primer*, which was an effort to provide some basic information on the process of having children through gestational surrogacy in the United States. In writing this new book, *Gestational Surrogacy: The Definitive Guide*, my goal is to provide a more comprehensive and definitive guide for intended parents and surrogates as they navigate the steps and stages through the surrogacy journey.

There are certain myths about gestational surrogacy in the United States, and my aim is to dispel these myths. For example, those who oppose gestational surrogacy may express an opinion that women who become surrogates are exploited, or that only wealthy people can afford to have children through surrogacy. Both arguments are misguided. Women who become surrogates in the United States are treated with respect, dignity, and gratitude. They are provided with independent legal counsel. They choose their own medical providers, and they make their own decisions regarding medical treatment as well as the compensation and reimbursements they receive. Further, parents from many walks of life have children through surrogacy. Yes, it is expensive, but the desire to have children is so fundamental for intended parents that they find ways to afford the process. Extended families assist and there are grants, loans and financing options through medical lenders and other financial institutions.

There are chapters in this book that outline costs and expenses. It should be noted that any monetary figures are representative of the suggested costs and expenses as of 2023, the year of this book's publication. These costs and expenses are increasing as the demand for surrogates is growing. Therefore, readers must check with their professional teams as to the specific costs and expenses that will apply to their surrogacy journeys.

For years, I have been consulting with intended parents, and representing both parents and surrogates in legal matters related to surrogacy. My purpose here is to take all the information that I have amassed in my years of experience as a lawyer and surrogacy advisor doing this work, and memorialize this information in this book, *Gestational Surrogacy: The Definitive Guide*.

PART I

Preparing for the Journey

1

The History of Gestational Surrogacy in the United States

The first distinction to be made when discussing the history of gestational surrogacy in the United States is the difference between traditional surrogacy and gestational surrogacy. This is because gestational surrogacy grew out of surrogacy in general. Before there was advanced medical technology such as successful in vitro fertilization (IVF), transfers of embryos created through IVF into the surrogate's womb, creation of embryos from egg donors and/or sperm donors, and other technological advances in reproductive medicine to achieve pregnancies, there was traditional surrogacy.

Traditional surrogacy is when the surrogate becomes pregnant with the sperm of the intended father. Her egg is fertilized, and she carries the pregnancy with the intention that the baby will be placed with the intended parents, and they will become the legal parents of this baby. The intended parents may be a heterosexual couple wherein the intended mother cannot conceive or become pregnant, a gay male or gay female couple, or a single intended father or single intended mother.

In these traditional surrogacy arrangements, although the surrogate Is agreeing to conceive and bear a child for the intended parents, the conception and pregnancy are the result of the fertilization of her egg. She is both the genetic mother and the birth mother.

Traditional surrogacy is also known as genetic surrogacy, and there are some current laws that provide for legal protection of intended parents and surrogates in cases where the surrogate is a genetic surrogate. One such law is the Connecticut Parentage Act, which allows genetic surrogacy and provides that the intended parents may petition a court of law to become the legal parents of the baby prior to the birth.

Traditional or genetic surrogacy is analogous to a woman who becomes pregnant and then allows the adoption of her baby by adoptive parents. The difference is that the parties to the traditional surrogacy agreement make the agreement prior to the pregnancy. They enter into a written agreement that states that the intended parents will become the legal parents of the baby, and the surrogate will relinquish her parental rights to the baby so that the intended parent(s) may become the legal parent(s) of the child.

One of the best-known contested cases in traditional surrogacy is *In the Matter of Baby M*, 109 N.J. 396, 525 A.2d 1128 (1988). In this case, a straight couple, the Sterns from Pennsylvania, contracted with Mary Beth Whitehead, a New Jersey woman. Their agreement stated that Mrs. Whitehead would become impregnated with Mr. Stern's sperm, and upon the birth of the baby, she would be paid $10,000 and give the baby to the Sterns, who would become the legal parents.

Upon the birth of the baby on March 27, 1986, Mrs. Whitehead changed her mind and wanted to keep her baby. A lower court ruled in favor of the Sterns and ordered that they have custody of the baby. The court terminated Mrs. Whitehead's rights. On appeal, the New Jersey Supreme Court reversed the lower court verdict and held that surrogacy contracts are unenforceable. Mary Beth Whitehead retained her maternal rights. However, the court awarded full custody to the Sterns and granted visitation rights to Whitehead.

There are also many traditional surrogacy cases with good outcomes. One gay couple asked the sister of one of the men to be their traditional surrogate. The sister was impregnated with the sperm of her brother's partner. She gave birth, willingly and happily delivered the baby to her brother and his partner, and relinquished her parental rights. The couple became the legal parents and continued to have an intact family. The birth mother transitioned into a very loving aunt.

The problem with the traditional surrogacy arrangement is the legal peril. Except in the cases of some current laws and legal procedures that must be carefully followed for legal protection, the baby is legally and ethically the child of the surrogate. If there are no laws to protect the intended parents, and if the intended parents do not retain legal counsel to carefully attend to the laws and procedures that may protect the intended parents, the traditional or genetic surrogate would have every right to change her mind and keep her baby.

Further, even if the few laws that might protect the intended parents are accessed, these laws are new and have not been tested in the courts. There is a possibility that genetic surrogacy laws may be found to be unconstitutional if ever fully tested by a genetic surrogate who desires to claim legal parentage for her genetic baby. The surrogate is conceiving, gestating, and giving birth to her own child.

Assuming there is a legal dispute over custody or legal parentage of the baby, the court will need to determine if the traditional surrogacy agreement is enforceable. The court may consider the expressed intentions of the parents as they are stated in the surrogacy agreement, but the court will scrutinize the agreement to determine if it meets the letter of the law or if there is some reason it may not be enforceable. Many judges may seek to side with the surrogate who is the genetic mother. There is most likely no case or lawyer that will be able to fully guarantee the intended parents of a traditional surrogacy arrangement that all will be legally safe or certain.

In fact, the *Baby M* case had a significant impact on surrogacy in the United States. As Sophie Lewis wrote, "[T]he case of *Baby M* immediately launched surrogacy into public infamy. In response to the drawn-out litigation and Supreme Court appeal that ensued, enormous crowds demonstrated up and down the east coast, and the Coalition Against Surrogacy was born."[1] The case highlighted the ethical dilemma posed by surrogacy in that it is often the exploitation of women in favor of more affluent people who can afford to hire someone to provide them with a baby. The concept of baby selling and the intensely strong and, in fact, important public policy against baby selling or baby buying is a prominent aftermath of the *Baby M* case. Iver Peterson wrote, "[T]o some who have studied the issue, one of the most disturbing elements of surrogate motherhood is the overtone of class exploitation."[2]

While many states and courts over the years made new laws to allow compensated gestational surrogacy, some states held on to strong public policies against any form of surrogacy. New York was one of those states. As an outcome of the *Baby M* case, New York enacted its Domestic Relations Law §123 (DRL §123), which "penalizes individuals who engage in surrogacy agreements for any remuneration." The law, now superseded, stated that a birth mother or her spouse, a genetic father and his wife, and, if the genetic mother is not the birth mother, the genetic mother and her spouse were subject to a civil penalty of up to $500 for attempting to enter into a surrogacy agreement. Further, any individual who assisted in arranging a surrogacy agreement for a fee was subject to a civil penalty of up to $10,000 for a first-time offense. However, in practice, an individual was permitted to pay for medical costs, which were considered reimbursement rather than compensation. Also, under the superseded New York law, if someone was penalized for arranging a surrogacy agreement, and violated the provision again, that individual could be found guilty of a felony.

At last, after years of attempts by legal experts and legislators in New York State, the Child Parent Security Act was passed in New York. On April 27, 2020, Denise Seidelman and Alexis Cirel, two attorneys who tirelessly spent years drafting, redrafting, and advocating the passage of this new law, reported in the *New York Law Journal,* "[O]n April 2, 2020, the Child-Parent Security Act (CPSA) passed the New York Legislature as part of Gov. Andrew Cuomo's year 2020 budget package. The CPSA is comprehensive, addressing and securing the legal relationship between children and their parents when the

---

1. S. Lewis, *Full Surrogacy Now: Feminism against Family* (London, UK: Verso Books), 30.

2. Iver Peterson, "Baby M, Ethics and the Law," *New York Times,* January 18, 1987, retrieved November 22, 2020, https://www.nytimes.com/1987/01/18/nyregion/baby-m-ethics-and-the-law.html.

children were conceived through third-party reproduction. The CPSA also discards New York State's antiquated ban on compensated gestational surrogacy, i.e., where the surrogate has no genetic relationship to the child."[3]

The New York Child Parent Security Act is a law that promotes the ethical practice of surrogacy more than any other law in the United States on the books at the time of this writing. It incorporates a Surrogate's Bill of Rights that provides statutorily based protections for women becoming surrogates including the following: (1) life insurance of $750,000; (2) comprehensive medical insurance to be paid for by the intended parents (with some exceptions) and to be maintained for twelve months after a birth, miscarriage, or termination of pregnancy; (3) the provision that women may make all of their health care decisions and choose their medical providers without a concern for breach of contract since this right is according to the statute; and (4) the right to terminate the surrogacy agreement for any reason at any time prior to a pregnancy. There are also many protective provisions for intended parents, including that they may file for a judgment of legal parentage directly after the surrogacy agreement is executed, that the surrogacy agreement is enforceable provided it includes the necessary elements from the new statute, and that the establishment of legal parentage is mandated if the statutory requirements are met.

Further, there is a clear description of what the compensation to the surrogate represents. There will not have to be guesswork by lawyers to figure out how to define or describe the compensation paid to surrogates. The New York CPSA (Article 5C of the Family Court Act) provides that "[c]ompensation may be paid to a donor or person acting as surrogate based on medical risks, physical discomfort, inconvenience and the responsibilities they are undertaking in connection with their participation in the assisted reproduction"[4]

Prior to the passage of the CPSA, although New York did not ban altruistic surrogacy (compassionate surrogacy), in which a woman agrees to gestate a child (not genetically related to her) for a couple or a single intended parent, the ban still had the effect of foreclosing compensated surrogacy arrangements. Women in New York who wished to become a surrogate to help create a family and to also receive fair compensation for all that they would go through to do this were not able to become gestational surrogates. Intended parents from New York were forced to look for and match with surrogates from other states in the United States where gestational surrogacy was legal.

Other states have also acted to enable willing and deserving intended parents to access gestational surrogacy. The state of Washington also had a ban on compensation surrogacy until its new law, the Uniform Parentage Act, took

---

3. D. E. Seidelman, and A. L. Cirel, "The Child-Parent Security Act Is a Game Changer: Here's What You Need To Know," Law.com, *New York Law Journal*, April 27, 2020, retrieved November 23, 2020, https://www.law.com/newyorklawjournal/2020/04/27/the-child-parent-security-act-is-a-game-changer-heres-what-you-need-to-know/.

4. See Family Court Act, Article 5C, Part 5, Compensation (NY CPSA § 581-502).

effect on January 1, 2019, legalizing compensated gestational surrogacy. In 2018, New Jersey, where the *Baby M* case originated, ended its many years of a compensated surrogacy ban by enacting the New Jersey Gestational Carrier Agreement Act.[5] (See chapter 10 ("Stages of the Surrogacy Journey"), section b, and chapter 13, "The Laws of Gestational Surrogacy," for an overview of legal matters related to surrogacy.)

Surrogacy began to be known in the legal sense in the United States in the 1970s. A lawyer by the name of Noel Keane drafted the first surrogacy contract in the United States in 1976 and continued to draft surrogacy contracts and assist in surrogacy arrangements for as many as 600 babies, including *Baby M*, the child of Mary Beth Whitehead.

As a result of the legal complications and legal risk of traditional surrogacy arrangements, as well as the advances made in reproductive medical technology such as in vitro fertilization, egg donation, and sperm donation, the landscape of surrogacy has transformed largely to one of gestational surrogacy. Traditional surrogacy still exists today, but gestational surrogacy has taken root as the most popular and widespread form of assisted reproduction through surrogacy in the United States.

Although the one drawback of gestational surrogacy is the cost, there are good reasons people turn to this way of having a child through surrogacy. It is legally safe in that the intended parents can become the legal parents of their developing baby before the birth in most cases, although some states provide for a post-birth legal process to establish parentage. Also, the intended parents have control of making their own embryos, either with their own egg and sperm or with egg donors and/or sperm donors that they choose.

---

5. NJ Rev Stat § 9:17-65 (2018).

2

The Ethics of Gestational Surrogacy in the United States

Because of the ethical framework of surrogacy in the United States, the technological advancements of reproductive medicine, and the competent and dedicated lawyers and physicians who practice gestational surrogacy, the United States is one of the best places to go through a surrogacy journey. The medical technology is highly advanced, resulting in excellent pregnancy success rates, and intended parents will have security in knowing that there is clear law to protect their parental rights. Another major reason is the practice of ethics by the professional community engaged in gestational surrogacy.

Throughout the world, there is controversy over surrogacy. Whenever there are conferences in Europe for surrogacy professionals and intended parents, there are street protests against surrogacy. They arise from a school of thought that surrogacy causes the exploitation of women—that is, the use of women as gestational hosts for the benefit of affluent intended parents who can pay for the services of a surrogate. A further branch of this opposition holds that surrogacy commodifies the conception of babies and, therefore, lends itself to baby buying, selling, and even trafficking.

Interestingly and not surprisingly, conservative entities such as the Catholic Church team up with feminists in their opposition to surrogacy:

> The Catholic Church has opposed this practice since the late 1980s. With the document *Donum Vitae*,[6] the Vatican's Congregation for the Doctrine of the Faith first expressed its opposition to any form of in vitro fertilization in 1987. Surrogacy has been defined as "an objective failure to meet the

---

6. "Instruction on Respect for Human Life in Its Origin and on the Dignity of Procreation Replies to Certain Questions of the Day," Vatican, 1987, retrieved November 26, 2020, http://www.vatican.va/roman_curia/congregations/cfaith/documents/rc_con_cfaith_doc_19870222_respect-for-human-life_en.html.

obligations of maternal love, of conjugal fidelity and of responsible motherhood" because it creates "a division between the physical, psychological and moral elements" that lead to the creation of a family.[7]

Some feminists also oppose surrogacy. "[I]t is not uncommon to see opposition from the left. In France, for instance, the country's largest lesbian association, the Coordination Lesbienne, has opposed surrogacy since 2011, and progressive feminists like the philosopher Sylviane Agacinski have joined the cause. In Sweden, it was a social democratic government—one that prided itself on being 'the first feminist government in the world'—that banned surrogacy in 2016. Spain's Feminist Party has also objected to it." However, "[n]ot all European feminists reject this practice: In Italy, for instance, Se Non Ora Quando—Factory, a group that split from Se Non Ora Quando over this issue, supports surrogacy, arguing that 'the desire of becoming a mother and a father has acquired new meanings.'"[8]

Notably, in the state of New York, as recently as 2019 (a time when forty-seven US states had already legalized compensated gestational surrogacy), feminists, including Gloria Steinem, spoke out against the Child Parent Security Act, a proposed law that would legalize compensated surrogacy in New York: "Women's rights scholars have argued that paid surrogacy turns women's bodies into commodities and is coercive to poor women given the sizable payments it can bring."[9]

Sadly, this view of surrogacy as it is practiced in some parts of the world is not altogether false. The argument that, in some places in the world where surrogacy arrangements are made, there is an exploitation of poor women as well as a lack of ethical practices is a legitimate argument.

In India, surrogacy practices include large houses or "hospitals" where pregnant surrogates are housed until they give birth. The intended parents usually do not meet their surrogates and the surrogates are subject to the rules of the clinic, the medical treatment that the clinic provides, and the housing that the clinic deems appropriate. The surrogates are separated from their families, and they have little or no say in the process. They do not choose the parents for whom they carry a baby. They do not make choices about their medical treatment or their housing while they are pregnant.

In her book *Surrogacy for All: Feminism against Family,* Sophie Lewis states, "[A]dequate medical care for postpartum surrogates (certainly in India, Romania, Mexico, and Guatemala) is horrifyingly absent. Lack of informed consent

---

7. A. Momigliano, "When Left-Wing Feminists and Conservative Catholics Unite," *The Atlantic,* March 28, 2017, 3, retrieved November 26, 2020, https://www.theatlantic.com/international/archive/2017/03/left-wing-feminists-conservative-catholics-unite/520968/.

8. Momigliano, "When Left-Wing Feminists," 3.

9. V. Wang, "Surrogate Pregnancy Battle Pits Progressives against Feminists," *New York Times,* June 12, 2019, retrieved November 27, 2020, https://www.nytimes.com/2019/06/12/nyregion/surrogate-pregnancy-law-ny.html.

appears depressingly endemic outside of the United States: workplace ethnographers from Bucharest to Bangalore have found that 'most surrogates do not understand what surrogacy really entails.'"[10]

In Thailand, commercial surrogacy is prohibited. The ban on surrogacy was put into place soon after the *Baby Gammy* case. In this case, a commissioning couple from Australia conceived twins with the help of a Thai gestational surrogate. During the pregnancy, it was discovered that one of the twins had Down's syndrome. The intended parents wanted to terminate the pregnancy, but the surrogate did not want to undergo a termination, as it was against her religious beliefs. Further, abortion was not legal in Thailand except in cases where the life of the mother was in danger, or the pregnancy was the result of a sex crime. The intended parents took custody of the healthy baby girl but abandoned their son, who was born with Down's syndrome.

It would be overly simple to look at the *Baby Gammy* case and just react to condemn surrogacy because such an outcome is even possible. However, it is more instructive to view the case in a way that would serve to improve upon the practice of surrogacy to make sure that such an occurrence will not happen again. There are ways in which a case like that of *Baby Gammy* might be avoided. With proper foundational work by the professionals working on behalf of the intended parents and the surrogate, the parties to the arrangement may be screened and matched on the basis of what they each believe they would and could do regarding abortion in the case of a birth defect. Also, the intended parents should have been trying to have a baby through surrogacy in a country where their wishes for a termination would have been at least legal, which was not the case in Thailand.

In stark contrast to these other countries where surrogacy arrangements are ethically questionable at best, the practices in the United States, monitored and discussed by professional organizations, lawyers, physicians and mental health providers, emphasize and advocate ethical practices in surrogacy. For example, the Society for Ethics in Egg Donation and Surrogacy (SEEDS) "is a nonprofit organization founded by a group of egg donation and surrogacy agencies, whose purpose is to define and promote ethical behavior by all parties involved in third party reproduction." This organization was founded and continues to thrive with over 100 members, including reproductive clinics, surrogacy and egg donation agencies, lawyers, and other professionals working in the field of surrogacy. The express purpose of SEEDS is to promote ethical standards for the practice of surrogacy and egg donation in the United States.

In the United States, surrogates come to the process voluntarily in every way. They participate in all the decisions regarding the surrogacy journey, including choosing their intended parents, choosing their medical care, and having rights to decline medical care. They live at home with their families during their pregnancies, and they choose whom they will have in the birthing room. They have independent legal counsel to ensure fair gestational

---

10. Lewis, *Full Surrogacy Now*, 32.

surrogacy agreements that include fair compensation for the disruption in their lives, the risks they are taking, and the expenses they incur because of engaging in a surrogacy journey.

In addition, in the United States, great care is taken to screen gestational surrogates and intended parents so that, when they are matched, they have the same ideas, beliefs, and perspectives on how the pregnancy will be managed. Of course, the surrogate has her own life, and she makes decisions about where she lives, what she eats, and which doctors she sees. But she also gets to know her intended parents. With the help of trained professionals, these people are matched and come together to bring a baby into the world. They are matched because they share similar views on what will happen under various circumstances that relate to the pregnancy, the health and well-being of the surrogate, and the health of the developing fetus. (See chapter 5, "Who Becomes a Gestational Surrogate?" and chapter 7, "The Work of the Surrogacy Agency," for details on matching.)

Moreover, the feminists' logic has little to no merit because the true feminist perspective argues for a woman's autonomy when it comes to making decisions for her own body. A woman should have choices: the choice whether to terminate a pregnancy without governmental interference as well as the choice whether to become pregnant as a surrogate and to be compensated for what she goes through as a surrogate helping to create a family.

3

First Thoughts and Considerations for Intended Parents

Planning to Have Children

The truly wondrous aspect of people having children through assisted reproduction is that these parents must seriously consider and deliberate bringing children into their lives. They are preparing for the difficult job of parenting, and they are bringing wanted children into the world. As Peg Streep points out, "[T]he decision to become a parent is a weighty one that should be made as consciously as possible. I say that not only as an unloved daughter who has listened to hundreds and hundreds of stories from children who were not, in the truest sense, loved by their mothers or fathers, but also as someone who had decided not to have children and then, nearing age 40, reversed herself. I now consider motherhood the crowning achievement of my life—and for a feminist, this is quite a statement."[11]

For many people, the desire to have children is a powerful urge that is deep-rooted and primal. Bonnie Rochman has written an article entitled "'Baby Fever' Is a Real Emotion, and Men Get It Too." In it, she states, "[I]f at some point you've had an irrepressible, inexplicable urge to make a baby, you may be interested to know there's a term for that—baby fever—and that it's a bona fide physical and emotional phenomenon."[12]

People who have to plan so intensely to have their children through alternative and assisted reproduction deserve a society that supports them and honors the fact that they will be doing their best to raise children who will

---

11. Peg Streep, "6 Terrible Reasons for Anyone to Have a Child," Psychology Today, December 1, 2015, retrieved December 11, 2020, https://www.psychologytoday.com/us/blog/tech-support/201512/6-terrible-reasons-anyone-have-child.

12. Bonnie Rochman, "'Baby Fever' Is a Real Emotion, and Men Get It Too," Time, September 6, 2011, retrieved December 11, 2020, https://healthland.time.com/2011/09/06/baby-fever-the-desire-to-procreate-is-not-just-for-women/.

become contributors and assets to society and culture. Each person's road to parenthood is different, but each person deserves the best and most compassionate medical, legal, and psychological support through their complex and emotional journeys to create their families.

Gestational surrogacy in the United States is a complex road that includes many steps, and sometimes, hurdles. Despite the complexity, though, it is a tried-and-true path to parenthood that many intended parents have successfully navigated. The key is to choose and be surrounded by experienced and competent professionals. The team will include a reproductive physician (reproductive endocrinologist a/k/a fertility specialist), attorneys, and psychologists and/or social workers. This is the group, together with nurses and administrators, that will be the foundational support for the intended parents and the gestational surrogate to bring a baby into the world.

One of the most important aspects of gestational surrogacy is that it can be (and will be) a very fulfilling, exciting, and joyful journey. People come together to join in a very intimate and amazing lifetime endeavor that involves conception, birth, and placing a newborn into the arms of his or her parents.

What to Do to Begin

Having a child begins with a desire to have a baby, to have children, and to create a family. Although there are people who wish to remain child-free, there are many people who desire to have children.

For many, having a child is a natural process that does not require assisted reproductive medical intervention. For others who desire to have children, it is not that simple. For various reasons, they need the medical technology of assisted reproduction. They must make a detailed plan to get pregnant, and the plans range from fairly simple circumstances, such as a lesbian choosing to be inseminated at a medical clinic with the sperm of a sperm donor, to the most complex, such as a couple or single individual needing to use an egg donor and/or sperm donor and a gestational surrogate to realize the dream of having a baby.

The many intended parents who have suffered from infertility, or who are LGBTQ+ intended parents must start by gathering information, educating themselves, and beginning to formulate a plan by which they will create their families.

How do people become parents? One path is sex between a man and a woman. His sperm enters her body at a time when her egg is leaving her ovary and traveling down her fallopian tube. The sperm find the egg in the fallopian tube. One of the millions of sperm penetrates the egg, and there is fertilization. The fertilized egg travels into the woman's uterus, implants itself into the uterine lining, and begins to grow. This is the embryo that grows into a fetus in the woman's womb, and finally becomes a newborn baby.

Sometimes, after sex, the sperm and egg do not connect to achieve fertilization, or the sperm and egg connect but the fertilized egg does not survive. There are many reasons for this including low sperm count or low sperm motility, or the eggs might be from a woman who is close to or has passed prime child-bearing years and does not have the hormone levels to produce viable eggs. In these cases, the couple might turn to IVF (in vitro fertilization), which is a process done in a reproductive medical clinic. A physician retrieves eggs from the woman's body and attempts fertilization outside the human body. Once fertilized, the resulting embryos are inserted with a catheter into the woman's uterus. See Chapter 14, "Reproductive Medicine and Gestational Surrogacy," for a more in-depth review of medical procedures related to assisted reproduction.

People who suffer from infertility also include women who have had hysterectomies (surgical removal of their uterus), men who have been ill and, as a result, cannot produce sperm to fertilize eggs. And there are LGBTQ+ people and single individuals who desire to create a family. These people must turn to different forms of assisted reproduction, such as egg donation, sperm donation, and/or gestational surrogacy.

Gestational surrogacy in the United States is a costly and complicated process. The gestational surrogacy process is called a journey for good reason. The first step is to say that you want to go on this journey. Second, you learn about the journey as it has been taken by many before you. Read about the process and talk to friends, family, or coworkers who have been on the journey. Perhaps attend counseling sessions with psychologists or social workers who specialize in fertility matters. Most importantly, if you are in a relationship and planning to take the journey with your partner, discuss and deliberate carefully and intimately what this will be like for you to do this together. Plan to make compromises and prepare to talk about difficult topics, such as how to finance the journey and what will happen if there are frustrations or hurdles along the way. Make a commitment to work things out together for the good of both of you. If you are single, discuss your plans with a trusted friend or family member. You don't have to announce your plans to everyone. But having a solid support system will be important to share the happy times and get through the challenging times with support and care.

Even in the best and most sound and satisfying relationships, challenges may arise that will cause tension and some disagreement in what options or solutions to pursue. Meeting with a competent and trained therapist or counselor may assist the intended parents in uncovering potential sources of disagreement and help them to prepare with strategies to successfully navigate concerns and issues that arise. The stronger the foundation for the journey, the more successful, positive, and happy the journey will be.

Once the decision is made to pursue gestational surrogacy to have children, the intended parents must begin to gather information about what is entailed in a surrogacy journey. It is a complex process that involves social, psychological, medical, and legal aspects, and each of these should be explored.

How do intended parents gather information? The Internet is useful to obtain resources but should not be relied upon for accurate information. People who post and publish on the Internet may have good intentions and publish useful information. However, laws, medical processes, and techniques change, so information may be outdated or inaccurate. Therefore, it is imperative for intended parents to have person-to-person consultations with lawyers and physicians to better understand the process and educate themselves on medical options and procedures, legal matters, the process and steps of gestational surrogacy, and costs.

Another way to gather information is to attend conferences that provide resources and information on creating families through alternative reproduction. Conferences, seminars, and workshops all over the world present information on surrogacy. Presentations on alternative family building are also offered by various groups and organizations.

Another method of gaining insight and information is to talk to parents who have already taken the journey and who have had their children through surrogacy. This is a way of finding out firsthand what went right as well as what was difficult. Keep in mind, though, that every surrogacy journey is different. There are married and unmarried couples who want to be intended parents, single intended mothers, single intended fathers, gay and straight couples. There are individuals and couples who have suffered years of infertility treatments, turning to surrogacy as a last hope, and there are intended parents who have had illnesses such as cancer, heart disease, and genetic conditions that leave them in need of a gestational surrogate to carry their baby.

The goal is to gather information but also to maintain the realistic perspective that your journey is your own and will not be like anyone else's. Why does this matter? It's true that the steps are similar for each journey, but people and circumstances are different. How you relate to the woman who is your surrogate, what thoughts and desires will go into your choice of a surrogate, and how you will approach creating embryos, choosing your professional team, and experiencing the pregnancy and birth will be different from anyone else's experiences.

Consultations with professionals such as physicians, lawyers, and surrogacy agency administrators are crucial in terms of deciding on the professional team. Intended parents need to feel the fit is right to move ahead with a professional team. Intended parents must seek out experienced, knowledgeable, and compassionate professionals with track records of helping many people in having their children through gestational surrogacy.

The team concept is critical. Surrogacy involves a group of people who come together to bring a baby into the world. The intended parents and the surrogate, and the surrogate's spouse or partner if she has one, come together and form the nucleus of the group bringing the baby into the world. The professional team, consisting of the reproductive physician, clinical staff, lawyer, surrogacy agency case manager, and support staff surround and support the nuclear group to provide critical and necessary foundational assistance to successfully navigate the surrogacy journey.

Who Turns to Gestational Surrogacy to Have Children?

Profiles of Intended Parents

Here are stories and essays in their own words from some of the many parents who have turned to gestational surrogacy.

B and H

We have been together for ten years, and we are both originally from Hungary, but we have been living in Amsterdam for eight years. We recently became Dutch citizens. H completed his studies here in the Netherlands. Having a passion for cooking, he had also worked as a chef in a Mexican restaurant during his studies, and after his recent graduation, he started working at the Dutch Media Institute as an archivist. At the same time, he is doing an internship at the Dutch Opera and Ballet as an archivist intern. B studied literature and cultural anthropology and currently works as a lecturer on arts and culture at Erasmus University. He will soon finish his PhD dissertation.

We met when we were still living in Hungary. It was love at first sight and, after being together only a few months, we moved to the Netherlands, partly because we wanted to experience living in another country and because B wanted to finish, and H wanted to start, his studies here. We immediately fell in love with the country, the openness of the people, the canals, and the parks of Amsterdam, with cycling as the main means of getting around, and more generally, with the relaxed and friendly atmosphere of everyday life, so we decided to stay here. Although the first months were sometimes challenging, we were always there to support each other, and we made some great friends, too. During the years we also learned Dutch, got jobs, bought a nice flat with many beautiful plants on our roof terrace, and adopted our cat, whose name is Laica. And while Amsterdam became our second home, we often go back to Hungary to spend the summer and winter holidays there with our friends and family, and they also regularly visit us.

In this respect, one of the greatest and most special moments of our life so far was our wedding in 2011: more than thirty friends and relatives traveled from Hungary to Amsterdam to celebrate with us. And we had a genuinely do-it-yourself wedding: some of the participants prepared a potluck dinner or baked the cake; others provided live music and performances. This way, everyone contributed and felt part of the event. We went on our honeymoon to Paris, and since then, we go back to Paris every year for a couple of days to celebrate our anniversary, and we always dream about continuing this tradition with the new addition(s) to our family in the future. Because we didn't have a lot of money when we first visited Paris, we just regularly bought bread, cheese, and wine and ate on the bank of the river instead of spending our money in expensive restaurants. And still, we keep this more romantic and cost-effective tradition when traveling. Two years ago, we explored Israel by backpack, and last year we traveled to New York and were able to visit B's cousins in Los Angeles. This year we decided to spend more time in Hungary and explore the Balaton (a wonderful lake with amazing natural scenery) with bikes.

While we love traveling and exploring new places, we equally enjoy the routines of daily life. We are passionate about our jobs, but over the years, we also adopted the philosophy "Work to live; don't live to work." We are very lucky that our jobs give us a lot of flexibility in this respect. In our free time, we go on long walks or spend time gardening on our terrace. H's main hobbies are theater and cooking, B plays the piano and paints. We both have an inherent drive to make our environment warm and homey. And although we love our current place, we are thinking about moving out of the city when we have children to have more space and to be closer to nature.

We very much enjoy spending time with the children of our friends and family members. Probably it is Lasha, a friend`s daughter who is the closest to our heart—she is already four, but we were already babysitting her when she was three weeks old. Every time we have kids around us, not only does our desire to become parents grow but such occasions also help us to picture how we will be (or how we would like to be) as parents. Most likely it is a learning process, which requires patience and consistency, and yet, at the same time, flexibility, probably a good sense of humor, and above all, unconditional love. Our relationship, which is based on honesty, empathy, and sharing, and our journey, as a couple, makes us more confident every day that we can provide these things to our future child or children to help her, him, or them to become happy individual(s).

A and L

Hello! We are L and A. A is a certified public accountant and received both his bachelor's and master's degrees from Rutgers University. I am a pediatric occupational therapist and received my bachelor's and master's degrees from Ithaca College in upstate New York. We have been married for four years and live just outside New York City in Westchester County. A and I enjoy traveling.

Some of our favorite places are Hawaii, Costa Rica, Italy, and Greece. When we are not exploring faraway places, we enjoy going to the beach, going to the movies, trying new restaurants, seeing Broadway shows in the city, and spending time with our family. We are fortunate to have both sets of parents, our siblings, and a niece and a nephew nearby, whom we enjoy seeing often. We believe that part of the success of our marriage is due to our supportive and complimentary personalities. A is more outgoing, while I am more introverted and observant.

Early into our relationship, we had conversations about our love for children and one day having our own family. Due to an early diagnosis of polycystic ovary syndrome as a teenager, I always knew conceiving could be difficult, as this syndrome can often prevent ovulation and cause irregular cycles, making it challenging to become pregnant naturally. We began our journey to conceive shortly after we married, but after nearly a year, we sought assistance and testing from my OB-GYN, and soon after, a reproductive endocrinologist (RE). After working with the RE for three months, I became pregnant but, sadly, miscarried at eight weeks. We completed seven more cycles with various fertility medications but were unsuccessful. At this point, we decided to move to IVF. We were full of hope, expecting this all-in move would bring us our baby. We completed two egg retrievals and four frozen embryo transfers, but all the results were either negative or an early (chemical) miscarriage. Despite autoimmune and endometrial testing, acupuncture, various medications, and supplements, our journey of carrying a baby had come to an end. At this point, nearly four years had passed, and we had tried every option for me to carry the baby. Our doctor felt it was best for us to explore other options, leading us to surrogacy.

Our main goals include growing through marriage and starting our family. Our parents have been married for decades, so we hope to continue this tradition and provide a loving household for our children. We look forward to finding a great woman to match with in this surrogacy process.

A and P

We are both extremely caring and loving people. Our hearts are filled with love for our nieces and nephews, but we yearn to have our own child. We have undergone multiple IVI (intravaginal insemination) treatments and four IVF treatments. The whole process has been heartbreaking, but we are a strong couple who can lean on each other for support, comfort, and laughter through the toughest times. We both find comfort in prayer as well, and we believe that there is a special woman out there who can be a blessing in our lives and help us build our family. Our baby will be welcomed into a world of love, laughter, and creativity, and an enormous amount of Italian food, dancing, beach days, a tennis-loving grandma, a dad who can teach him or her to ski, and so much love and unconditional support.

A was an innkeeper on Nantucket for eleven years, and she was a manager with the Four Seasons Hotels group—making her an extremely patient person.

P is a real estate developer with a law degree, which makes him a person of perpetual sound mind and good advice. A feels that P always knows the right thing to do. Together, they form a team of two smart selfless individuals who will raise a child to always try to do the right thing, and to always think of others.

D

I was born into a large family in Ireland. There were thirteen children: six girls and seven boys. Though we grew up on a large farm, we struggled through difficult financial times and managed to put ourselves through college. As a graduate with an MBA in architecture from *** University, my career had centered on real estate development. Upon graduation, I worked for six years in London before immigrating to New York in 1990, where my work focused on building skyscrapers. The financial crisis of 2008 hit the real estate industry particularly hard, and I found myself unemployed. So I decided to travel the globe and succeeded in visiting every country on the planet. I returned to the United States in 2012 and was hired by *** to develop their campus in India. After my assignment in India, I returned to the United States in 2014 and have continued in real estate development.

I have an interest in children, and I have a lot of experience with them. I have thirty-five nieces and nephews with diverse ethnicities. I have decided that, after achieving all my goals in life, it is time to have a family of my own.

At this moment in my life, I am financially secure and held in high esteem in my career. I have a fascination with the fields of anthropology and global politics. I am educated in many venues with an involvement in mentoring and student placements.

I am single. I have many friends and a good strong support system. I lean toward friends of diversity and broad experiences. I have no vices such as alcohol, drugs, or cigarettes. I am told that I have a quick and sharp wit and can get people to smile instantly.

After very serious consideration and talking to many friends who have been through the surrogacy process, I have been encouraged by all to take the leap into parenthood. There have been no regrets or second thoughts upon making this momentous decision.

T and J

My name is T, and my husband's name is J. If you are reading this, it means that you are considering giving us an extraordinary gift. Until we can speak and get to know each other directly, we hope this brief introduction will give you a sense of who we are.

We met eleven years ago, and we were married three years later. Our wedding ceremony was in the same church where I had been baptized and received First Holy Communion and Confirmation. We immediately made plans to start a family. Unfortunately, I suffered four miscarriages over the next few years. Throughout all our despair, we never really considered abandoning our dream of having children. Now, we seek a miracle with your help.

We would love to be parents and be given the opportunity to love and nurture a child from birth. We realize how incredibly precious a surrogate mother is, and we want our child to know about you. Our child will have a fun, loving home with two parents who love each other. We have a four-bedroom home, with a large backyard and a pool, in a lovely neighborhood with lots of children. Down the block is a duck pond in a large, quiet park.

I am self-employed, which allows me the luxury of a flexible schedule and the ability to work from home. After graduating from college, my mother asked me to help her start a medical billing company. My sister joined the business two years later, and we now run the business together since Mom has retired.

J is a pilot and a great handyman around the house. He is incredibly loyal and loving. He is my best friend.

J says, "T is the love of my life. She is intelligent, witty, and very hard working. She is the best wife a man could imagine and will be the best mother a child could ask for." He also states, "I always wanted to be a pilot since I was a child. After many years in the music industry, I decided to go back to college for aeronautics and take flying lessons. The rest is history."

We are very close to our families. My parents, sister, brother-in-law, and niece, H, live close by. H is twelve years old, and she enjoys horseback riding. She owns a beautiful white horse named Chrissy. In fact, she inspired me to take horseback riding lessons. J's family is just a short drive or train ride. His niece just finished her first year of college, and his nephew is going away to college next year. We often spend the holidays and special occasions together. We are looking forward to a summer vacation with J's family this year and lots of fun times on my family's boat.

We offer all the love we have with a secure family unit and financial situation.

For us, there would be no greater joy than parenthood. Thank you for considering us.

A and J

Before we tell you a bit about ourselves, we first and foremost want to thank you in advance for everything you will do to help us bring our child into the world. We cannot even express to you how appreciative we are and how fortunate we feel to have found you.

These past few years have been filled with so much good in many ways, but they have also come with many moments of unbearable heartbreak. We have suffered multiple miscarriages as we tried naturally to become pregnant and underwent painful surgical procedures and five cycles of IVF, only to suffer additional miscarriages. During our long journey, there were times when we felt that the child that we wanted so badly, and had tried so hard to conceive, would never come.

As a last effort, we ended up turning to surrogacy, and finally, we were most fortunate to welcome our son, F, into the world, earlier this year! F has been a wonderful blessing and our greatest dream come true. He is such a sweet little boy, and we could not be more grateful. Our new hope is that we will be able to continue to grow our family. We would be so excited to be able to give F a sibling to go through life with.

Now, to introduce ourselves: We are a married couple from New York. We first met eleven years ago after being introduced by A's older brother. We hit it off immediately. We had so many things in common; we shared interests, core values, and long-term goals; and, as it turned out, we also had quite a few mutual friends. Some of our siblings had even overlapped in high school. We couldn't believe we had never met before!

We fit perfectly. A is fun and sweet and amazingly creative. She is the ultimate optimist and always has a smile on her face. J is smart and thoughtful, hardworking, and caring, with a good heart and an ability to put anyone at ease. He works in finance.

We both love food, movies, and art. We spend our weekends exploring the city and taking advantage of all it has to offer, visiting museums, discovering new neighborhoods, checking out new restaurants, and spending time with family and friends, who are so crucial to our lives. We cannot wait to do these same things with all our children one day, and we hope that we can instill in them a constant curiosity and passion for life.

We both come from large, very close families—A is one of four, and J is one of three—and there is nothing more important to us than creating a family of our own. Our parents are incredibly supportive: they have been there for us and will continue to be there for us, every step of the way, and want nothing more than to see us grow our own family.

Before we were fortunate to have been blessed with F, we had wanted to be parents for what felt like forever, and each pregnancy loss was immensely hard on our hearts, but now that we have F, we realize, on another level, what we would have missed without someone like you. We are so in awe of you, your selflessness, and your generosity in helping us in our struggle to have children. We are very excited for the next steps and very much look forward to the possibility of you coming on this journey with us.

A and M

We are very excited about this upcoming surrogacy journey, which comes after a long, exhausting, and disappointing time of trying to have babies. Let's tell you something about us. We are A and M, both thirty-three years old. Nine years ago, A was traveling as a student from Germany to Israel, where she met M on the campus . . . and our story starts there. We were able to overcome all boundaries regarding our multicultural and geographical differences, convincing all our friends and family from the beginning that we are what will be. After being in a long-distance relationship for two years, A moved to Israel, living with M in Tel Aviv. Two years later, we decided to move back to Germany, where we have lived in Berlin for the last five years. We got married four years ago, looking forward to building a big family together. We take pride in sharing the same family values and approach to life, seeing family as the most important thing.

After not being successful naturally, we started intensive fertility treatments almost three years ago. We were very discouraged, putting all our efforts into the process, which was not fruitful and was without a discovered medical reason. Finding out about surrogacy in the United States gave us new hope, as our embryos are not considered the problem and surrogacy is not an option in Germany.

We would describe both of our personalities as positive, usually optimistic, and communicative. We are happy and like to laugh and be surrounded by many friends. If one of us is having difficulties, the other always lifts that one's spirits up, so our periods of being sad or disappointed are usually very short. Both of us love kids and are loved by all the kids of our friends surrounding us, being their additional "uncle" and "auntie."

A works at the University Hospital of Berlin. M is a financial analyst. We both like our jobs but also enjoy the times we are not at work. We enjoy spending time with friends, cooking together, doing sports such as running and playing squash, and from time-to-time practicing playing the piano. We love traveling in nature and in different countries, learning and experiencing foreign cultures. Between us we speak three languages, but mainly English since this is how we met.

We are ready to step up to the next stage of life, waiting to share all our interests and love with our kids and give them everything they need to be as happy as we have always been. We are looking forward to the surrogacy process and feel very lucky and a little nervous being able to travel that route.

CB

Since I was a young child who grew up in a large family of modest means in a small town where most never went to college, I wanted to be a doctor and have a practice in New York City as well as take care of some of the poorest people in the world. Through hard work and determination, I excelled in high school, put myself through college and medical school, and was admitted to one of the top hospital training programs in the world.

I believe that almost anything is possible if you want it badly enough in life. This philosophy has gotten me much in life, for which I am grateful. I also have always believed that it is extremely important to give back where you can and remember where you came from. Over twenty years, I have built a medical practice affiliated with one of the country's largest academic medical institutions. I have helped build charity hospitals, schools, and women's centers in the poorest regions of India and Nepal.

I have enjoyed mentoring and teaching hundreds and hundreds of medical students and doctors in training over my career. Helping foster new students and doctors in an academic environment is a wonderful way for me to give back and to also continue my own learning.

Life obviously cannot be all work and no play. I have a great love of travel and have been to nearly 100 countries, always trying to learn about other cultures and people. I spend time reading and going to the movies. I enjoy sports, both playing them and watching them. I especially like biking, hiking, and other outdoor activities. I come from a large family, with thirteen nieces and nephews, all of whom I have been intimately involved with in their lives for close to thirty years. Family is extremely important to me, and I have wanted to build my own for a very long time but wanted to wait until I was well established and would have more time to spend with my future children and raise them myself as much as possible. Now is that time and I am so excited to begin this journey!

M and R

We are a gay couple who have just as much fun now as we did when we met twenty years ago. Over the years, one of the only things missing from our amazing lives was a child. It's now a possibility for us, and we are excited beyond belief to start an exciting new chapter for our family. We grew up in Virginia and moved up to the NYC area in 2002 once M graduated from college. At first, it was a major adjustment period being in such a different environment, but over the years, it became home. At one point, R moved back to Virginia for work, and we both dealt with a long-distance relationship for four years, which was difficult, to say the least. Through it all, we kept our eye on the prize of being together under one roof once again. The issue always was that M could only do his job in the fashion industry around NYC, and it was much more difficult for R to find a job in his industry, and in such a competitive media market as NYC. Finally, in early 2009, an opportunity came up in the suburbs of NYC, and we moved to the bucolic surroundings of Connecticut. It was the perfect choice for us both as we love the peacefulness and serenity of the suburbs but also thrive on the energy and culture of the city. M loves commuting each day, as he gets both experiences daily. It pretty much sums up how we'd like to raise our child, getting the best of both worlds. Since we both grew up in the Virginia suburbs, we'd also like the same for our child or children. It's important to us that the child not only knows the safety and routine of good schools, sports teams, and neighborhoods but also appreciates the diversity, culture, and energy of the city.

M has identical twin brothers who are fourteen years younger than he is (yes, he was an only child until he was a teenager). He grew up very close to his uncles, aunts, cousins, and grandparents, who were single-handedly responsible for exposing him to things such as nice restaurants, travel to different cities, and an appreciation for hard work. He remains close to them to this day. M's mom and dad were younger parents, which was an amazing asset growing up, since his mom took such an interest in everything in his life. Both of our moms are ecstatic about becoming grandmas as this child will be their first! Most of our families still live in Virginia or very close to there.

We both have very interesting jobs, a fact that always makes for great dinner conversation with our friends. No two days are typically the same, something that we love. Both of us are born communicators. We love meeting people, having a close circle of good friends (many of whom also have young kids), and, most importantly, laughing every single day.

We are 100 percent committed to having a household full of love, laughter, and positivity. There isn't one day that doesn't go by that, as a couple, we aren't silly in some way. It's an essential juxtaposition to the intensity of daily life, and it's something we'll absolutely make sure our child is exposed to as well. We love traveling to places in the summer such as North Myrtle Beach in South Carolina (something our families have done our entire lives), as well as a few trips to some of our favorites, such as Martha's Vineyard and Miami. We've spent years loving to watch dads and their kids play in the pool and on the beach, and we cannot wait to do the same with ours. We are looking forward to making traditions for our family! Finally, the excitement of starting our family cannot fully be expressed in this essay. We have worked so hard to get to this point to make it a possibility, and we truly look forward to having a great relationship with our surrogate and her family in the years ahead. We don't look at this as a simple nine-month process. Rather, we are searching for an amazing woman whose role in our family will go beyond the pregnancy and birth.

C and R

Hi! We are C and R. We live in a beautiful town in Connecticut that is perfect for raising a family. We have been married for almost nine years and went on our first date ten years ago. Our families have been friends for over thirty years, and they are the ones who set us up! We both come from close families who all live within a few minutes of each other. We have a strong support system of family and friends. We were blessed to adopt our daughter in May of 2015. We loved her from the moment we laid eyes on her. She is a sweet, kind, funny, smart, and caring four-year-old. She loves children and wants to hug every child she sees! We are so excited about expanding our family through surrogacy. It has been a very difficult period of several years as we navigated infertility and trying to adopt again. The last two and a half years have been filled with multiple adoption scams and a failed adoption at the time of birth, so at this time we believe surrogacy is our best option to expand our family.

C says about R: R is the quintessential example of a perfect partner. He is caring, devoted, loving, and supportive. His dedication to our daughter and me is astonishing, and we are so lucky to have him in our lives. Education is very important to us. R has a bachelor's degree and is always reading to further educate himself. He is a business owner, which affords him the ability to make his own hours so that he is always available to our family. He works very hard so that we can travel as a family, send our daughter to the best school, and allow her to be involved in as many activities as she pleases. R loves to make us laugh. Whether it is a silly dad joke or a wacky dance, he knows how to make us smile. R will do anything to make our daughter happy. From playing with dolls to playing basketball, he does it all with her. He is an amazing father and the best friend I could have ever asked for.

R says about C: While I have known C for many years, watching her raise our daughter has deepened my love for her. C is the most thoughtful and caring person I have ever known. She is an incredibly warm and loving wife and mother. She fills our days with fun and lots of adventures. Everything she does is to make my life and our daughter's life special and memorable. I am so blessed to have found such a strong, nurturing, and caring wife. Before becoming a stay-at-home mom to our daughter, C was a physician's assistant (she has bachelor's and master's degrees). She plans to continue to be a stay-at-home mom. C loves to celebrate every holiday. She especially goes all out for Christmas. (We are known in the neighborhood for our holiday displays!) Our daughter likes to be a "big helper" and tell us where to put the decorations. Thank you so much for taking the time to learn more about us. We don't think there is any way to put into words what it would mean to us to have the opportunity to have another child.

J and N

We don't mean to suggest that this is the defining experience of our lives or our relationship, but as it relates to surrogacy, J's breast cancer seems the most logical place to start this introduction to who we are and what we're about:

J was diagnosed at twenty-eight years old during our first year of marriage. She did IVF, and we froze embryos almost immediately. After J underwent surgery and chemo and radiation and we then spent a year or so working to reestablish some normalcy in our lives, we started exploring how we could expand our family.

Doctors put J on ten years of hormone therapy to help ensure her cancer will not return. The drugs also prevent her from getting pregnant. J's best friend since grade school (who has three kids of her own) offered to carry our first child for us. Our friend gave birth to our daughter, L, in 2018. We fully recognize what an extraordinary act that was and what an unusual (and amazing!) surrogacy experience we had with our friend.

As for who we are, N is from an island off the Coast of Oregon. J grew up in a small town in Connecticut. We met and started dating while working as camp counselors, the summer after our sophomore year of college. We dated long distance. We broke up, and we got back together repeatedly in the years that followed, moving around from Maine and Pennsylvania to Chicago and Idaho, before reconnecting in New York City and getting married a few years later at the camp where we met. We've since moved out of the city to an old house in the woods of Connecticut and are working (slowly) to fix it up.

N is a reporter for a local TV station. J is a director of philanthropy at a large nonprofit organization. We're both very motivated and driven, but we're also maybe more aware of our mortality than others of our age. Because of that, I think we're definitely extra focused on quality of life, time with friends and family and pets (we have two white cats and a huge black dog), seeing the humor in life (even/especially during its darkest moments!), time outdoors, and enjoying each other (and L!) as much as we can.

We're both realists, but I'd also say we're pretty good at recognizing (and we look for!) the positives in our own lives, people, and the world around us.

MW

The happiest day of my life was the day I gave birth to my now eight-year-old daughter. I was forty-six years old at the time and about to turn forty-seven, and I had started trying to have my own child shortly after I turned forty years old. I remember feeling devastated when my physician told me I probably couldn't have my own biological child because of my age. But then she said I could consider using an egg donor. And my beautiful daughter came into this world because of the generosity of another woman. I became pregnant with my daughter with donor eggs from another, very kind woman, and my daughter is now a happy, healthy third grader.

I was married when I was twenty-five years old to a guy I fell madly in love with, but when it became clear the marriage wasn't going to work, I knew we shouldn't have children together. We divorced within two years, but because we still loved each other we kept seeing each other for another five years after our divorce. But that's when I learned that love alone is not enough to keep two people together. I decided then that I would build a good career so I wouldn't have to worry about whether I could afford to take care of a child on my own if I had to. I'd always wanted to be a mother, and ideally, I was hoping to find a good guy and get married again and then start a family. While I was building my career and pursuing first a master's degree and then a doctoral degree, I dated but didn't find that perfect guy. By the time I turned forty, I knew that if I wanted to be a mom, I couldn't wait for that perfect guy. I also knew that I was in a good position financially and emotionally to be a single mom. So, I started trying in 2009, and my angel came along two years later.

While my daughter is the love of my life, I still have more love to give and really want to be a mom again. In addition, even though I'm a single parent I have a solid and very supportive network of family and close friends, so if anything should happen to me, my family is already lined up to step in. I was raised by a single mom, and I'm very close to my two brothers. Most of my closest friends I met either while I was working or when I was in graduate school. The graduate school had a large international student body, so I made many friends who live all over the world. My daughter has two godmothers and one godfather, along with two uncles, an aunt, her grandmom, and several cousins, almost all of whom live in New York except for the godmothers. One lives in Africa, and the other is French and works internationally. She lives in whatever country she is currently working in.

My daughter attends private school, and any sibling of hers would have sibling priority for acceptance into the same private school. I was raised Christian, but I'm not a super-religious person. I pretty much believe God is love.

I'm currently a full-time college professor teaching economics, and I've been doing that for the last five years. The schedule allows me to be a very present and hands-on mom. I also love to travel abroad, partly because I have friends who live overseas, so my daughter and I usually have a place to stay when we travel, and partly because, due to my work, I frequently conduct presentations at academic conferences, some of which take place outside the United States. My daughter has already traveled with me to Brazil, Ghana, Ethiopia, and South Africa.

If you are reading this profile, I'd like to thank you very much for considering me as someone you might want to help. I'm sure you're an amazing person because the gift you're thinking about giving is incredible. I would be open to any kind of relationship you may like to have; it would be totally your call. I was blessed and lucky enough to have one child. There is nothing and no one that makes me happier than my daughter. I do hope you'll consider helping me bring another blessing into the world. I can assure you he or she would be so loved, so cherished. I would do all that I could to give the child the best life I could so that he or she, when the time comes, can go out and live the best life. Thank you so much for taking the time to read my profile.

T and S

Hi! We are T and S. We met in 2008 at a mutual friend's housewarming party. We are a couple who lives, laughs, loves, and works together! What started out as a chance encounter soon blossomed into a great romance. We took things slowly at first, but we knew we were soulmates, and, within a year of meeting, we were living together, and we got married in June of 2012. We had a beautiful wedding surrounded by friends and family.

S grew up as an only child. T grew up as one of five siblings. While we each had different experiences growing up, family has remained paramount for each of us. Both of us chose to pursue a communications degree at the same college. That's not the only similarity. Fun facts: S and T were both born on the fifth of the month, and both our moms were born on the seventeenth of the month, with each mom giving birth exactly fifty days after their own birthday! We were also in the Disney college program together, living in Orlando for a semester. Many people are astonished that we can live and work together. It takes a high degree of communication and compromise. We also give each other the space we need to pursue individual creative interests. T enjoys his photography hobby and is an avid musician, who sings every Tuesday night with his *a capella* group and who turned our new dining room into a music room complete with a baby grand piano. S enjoys collecting art and working on various craft projects. Together we enjoy cooking, watching *Homeland*, and decorating our home. We are so excited to grow our family, sharing all we have with the child or children we hope to be blessed with!

December 4, 2018, update from T and S: In January 2016, Worldwide Surrogacy found and paired us with an amazing gestational surrogate. She had been a gestational surrogate once before, for a gay couple, and had a loving husband

and two daughters of her own. For two years we built an incredible personal relationship with her and her family as we navigated the (sometimes rough) waters of the child creation journey. We maintain regular communications with her, not daily as we used to but enough to know what's going on in each other's lives. Our son was born at 9 a.m. on a Sunday morning in July 2018. The hospital was very close to our home, so we were there for the big moment. There's nothing on God's green earth that compares to childbirth. Hands down, it was the most emotional experience we've ever had. And we weren't even the ones pushing! Oh my gosh! Since then, life has been an endless adventure with our little guy. He's the light and love of our lives. We try so hard not to spoil him rotten and to give him a balanced life with challenges, playtime, reading time, social time, and travel. We love to travel, and so far, we refuse to slow down. In fact, our son had the pleasure of traveling to Greece in September with us, his two-year-old cousin, and eight of his favorite uncles. He even learned to walk at the Acropolis. The rocky ground wasn't conducive to crawling. Now that he's almost a year and a half, it's time to start the sibling journey. We would like to have a family of two or three children. We couldn't be more excited to start this next journey.

P and M

If you're reading this profile, we're already so lucky that you're considering us! We are so thrilled at the possibility of having a child, and we know our surrogate would be giving us the most important gift of our lives.

P is thirty-three and I'm thirty-five, and we live in Brooklyn, New York. I grew up in England (yes, I have an accent!) and moved to the United States in 2006. P grew up in Connecticut, and we met eleven years ago when I was in graduate school and P was in college. After we both finished school, we moved in together, and our first apartment was a tiny studio apartment that was only 425 square feet. I joke that we love each other now, but we must have *really* loved each other back then.

We got married in 2014 in New York on a very wintry day. Both our families were there to celebrate with us, and we're lucky to be very close to our parents and siblings. I have a younger brother who is an actor. P has an older sister and a niece. We included a photo of us with P's niece after making gingerbread houses last Christmas.

For many years, we knew that we wanted to start a family, and we've been working to get ready to provide the best environment for raising a child. We moved to an apartment in a good school district because education is very important to us. (P's mom was a public-school teacher, and so is his sister.) We also both changed jobs in the last few years so that when our family grows, we'll have more time together. I'm working as a lawyer and P works for the New York City government.

Between the two of us, we have a lot of (nerdy) interests. We're in a movie club and we go to trivia nights at our favorite local restaurant. In the summer, we like to go to the beach or to bike around the city. My idea of a great night is to have dinner at home with a few friends—P is a good cook and I do the washing up—followed by a couple of board games.

Our outlook on life is that you plan you want, but not everything goes according to plan and so you'd better enjoy the journey, too. I hope we will approach parenting in the same way, giving our child the best opportunities we can, but also creating a home full of laughter and joy.

How to Begin Gathering Information

Intended parents are unique and, therefore, the ways in which intended parents begin the search for information on gestational surrogacy will differ. Some are emerging from years of struggling with the losses, frustrations, and sadness of infertility. They may hear about the possibility of surrogacy from their reproductive physician. Some may talk about their desire to have a child and their need to explore alternative family formation, and they may hear about surrogacy from a friend or a relative. Others may be very private about the need to find an alternative family-building path, and they may turn to the Internet to do their initial research. There is a method of information gathering that will fit each intended parent's need.

This idea of privacy is critical. Having a child by means of an alternative method of family formation is difficult and intensely personal. While some parents may confide in family and friends and even look for support outside their closely held support system, other intended parents may desire to maintain confidentiality throughout the process until they have some measure of success, such as a healthy pregnancy or even a birth. It is important to know that consultations with lawyers and physicians are confidential. Such professionals, under their professional codes of ethics as well as laws such as HIPAA (Health Insurance Portability and Accountability Act),[13] are required to maintain the confidentiality of the information their patients and clients provide to them and what they discuss in terms of advice and planning. Records are kept confidential.

With respect to consultations with professionals, it is important that intended parents research the professionals to determine if they are reputable in the field of gestational surrogacy. Choosing someone off the Internet may work out but, equally, may lead to frustration and financial loss. Here are some ideas for research to obtain potential referrals to lawyers, agencies, and physicians before you meet with them:

1. If you have a reproductive physician you know and trust, ask him or her for referrals to surrogacy lawyers and surrogacy agencies.

---

13. See US Department of health and Human Services, "Your Rights under HIPAA." "The Privacy Rule, a federal law, gives you rights over your health information and sets rules and limits on who can look at and receive your health information. The Privacy Rule applies to all forms of individuals' protected health information, whether electronic, written, or oral. The Security Rule is a federal law that requires security for health information in electronic form," https://www. hhs.gov/hipaa/for-individuals/guidance-materials-for-consumers/index.html.

2. If you have a surrogacy lawyer that you know and trust, or you have heard of one who is considered to be reputable and trustworthy, ask this source for referrals to reproductive physicians.

3. If you have friends or relatives who have turned to surrogacy to have their children, ask them about their professional team and if they would use this team again. Ask them about the pros and cons of the professionals with whom they worked.

4. Check out organizations that have lists of professionals and even ratings and reviews such as Men Having Babies[14] or Go Stork.[15]

5. Find reputable attorneys by reviewing the directory of the Academy of Adoption and Assisted Reproduction Attorneys[16] or other professional directories.

These consultations with professionals are crucial for several reasons. First, if intended parents are meeting with a professional experienced in the field of gestational surrogacy, they will be getting information that is most likely based on experience and expertise. Second, they will be able to ask their specific questions, express their personal concerns, and receive direct answers and feedback. Third, the intended parents will have an opportunity to tell their story of how and why they are turning to gestational surrogacy. They will then have an opportunity to experience firsthand the response to their story and to feel and know if there is empathy, compassion, knowledge, confidence, and expertise coming from the individual physician, lawyer, or agency representative with whom they are consulting. This is crucial feedback because surrogacy is one of the most personal and complicated life endeavors that intended parents will find their way into, and they must build relationships based on information and trust.

Of course, one major factor is the experience and competence of the professional. Another major factor is the intended parents' trust and an intuitive knowledge that they will be in good hands, that they will be taken care of during this most intimate milestone of their lives.

Surrogacy is complex, but in the hands of experienced and expert professionals, it is very understandable and safe. Except for the natural mother-nature risks in IVF, pregnancy, and birth, risks are very minimal when intended parents and surrogates are under the care and guidance of a competent legal and medical team.

When preparing for consultations with professionals, intended parents should have their list of questions ready. No question is too simple or mundane when it comes to surrogacy, and that is a very good first clue to how you feel about doctors or lawyers with whom you are consulting. Do they answer questions with willingness and availability and without hesitation? Do they make

---

14. Men Having Babies, https://www.menhavingbabies.org/.

15. GoStork, https://www.gostork.com/.

16. Academy of Adoption and Assisted Reproduction Attorneys, https://adoptionart.org/.

you feel that your questions and concerns are important? Do they listen to your story so you feel that your case matters, that you will be an important and unique client or patient?

Here are some questions to start with when you meet with the surrogacy agency:

1. How long has your agency been in existence?
2. How many babies does your agency help bring into the world each year?
3. Does your agency provide legal assistance? If not, how are legal issues handled, and will a lawyer be available if we have legal questions?
4. How long does it take to be matched with a surrogate?
5. What are the reasons for the waiting time to be matched with a surrogate?
6. Can we get a surrogate within driving distance to us?
7. Can we get a surrogate with medical insurance to cover a surrogate pregnancy? If not, how much does medical insurance for a surrogate cost, approximately?
8. Who will help us or guide us to obtain insurance for our surrogate?
9. What kind of case management and support system does your agency provide for intended parents?
10. Will someone be available after business hours and on weekends if we need to speak to someone at the agency?
11. Do surrogates receive individual support during the journey?
12. What happens during the matching process?
13. How do you know if a surrogate will be a good match for us?
14. How do you screen surrogates? What is the screening protocol or process?
15. What US states do surrogates come from?
16. Why do women become surrogates?
17. How do you recruit your surrogates?
18. Should we have an experienced surrogate?
19. How do we know that the law in a state where we might be matched is good for us?
20. Do you screen the surrogates before the match commitment is made?
21. Do we choose our surrogate?
22. What information will we receive about a surrogate?
23. Does our reproductive physician review the proposed surrogate's medical records?
24. Are intended parents screened too?
25. What do intended parents have to do in terms of screening?
26. How often will our case manager contact us?
27. Will we see detailed information about the surrogate candidates proposed to us?
28. Are surrogates married? If so, how are their spouses involved?

29. What kind of a relationship will we have with our surrogate?

30. Can we go to prenatal appointments?

31. Can we be present at the birth?

32. Will we have access to the medical information and reports regarding the pregnancy?

33. How do they know at the hospital that we are the parents?

34. Will my surrogate want to keep my baby?

35. Have you ever had a contract dispute between a surrogate and intended parents? If so, how did you handle it?

36. What lawyer will represent us when we enter a gestational surrogacy contract?

37. What lawyer will represent the surrogate?

38. What are the fees and costs?

39. What is the compensation to the surrogate? How is that determined?

40. What if the surrogate does not get pregnant?

41. What if the surrogate has a miscarriage?

42. If she does not get pregnant, will we get another surrogate?

43. If we need another surrogate, how does that affect fees and costs?

44. Is there a rematch fee?

45. How long will it take to be matched with a second surrogate?

46. What happens if there is a birth defect?

47. Can we ask the surrogate to terminate the pregnancy if there is a serious birth defect?

48. What is a prebirth order? How will we become legal parents of our baby?

49. Will our names go on the birth certificate?

50. When will we get our baby's birth certificate?

51. Will you help us get a passport for our baby if we need one?

52. What is escrow management?

53. Do you have an escrow management system?

54. Do we have to use the agency's escrow management system, or can we have a choice?

55. What is the timing of having to fund our escrow account?

56. Will we know what is being paid out of escrow?

57. Is our money safe?

58. If there is money left after the birth, will it be returned to us?

59. How long after the birth do we have to wait for the return of our excess escrow funds?

60. What if we don't have an IVF clinic yet? Can you give us some recommendations?

61. Does the surrogate have to live near the IVF clinic?

62. Can we speak to any former clients about working with your agency?

63. What distinguishes your agency from other surrogacy agencies?

Next, here are some questions for the reproductive physicians. This list is as comprehensive as possible, and some of the questions may not be applicable to all intended parents. The goal is to review this list to be better prepared for the consultation:

1. Do you have experience doing gestational surrogacy arrangements and helping to get surrogates pregnant?
2. Approximately how many surrogacy arrangements do you do each year?
3. Do you work with surrogacy agencies?
4. Can you give us recommendations or a list of possible surrogacy agencies?
5. How do you medically screen the surrogates?
6. Do you do blood tests to check for drugs, alcohol, nicotine, and other issues, such as sexually transmitted diseases?
7. What medical information will you get on the proposed surrogate?
8. What should we look for in a surrogate?
9. Do surrogates have children?
10. Have you ever had a surrogate want to keep a baby?
11. Can we get medical information about the surrogate?
12. If she gets pregnant, will you share with us medical information about the pregnancy?
13. What are the steps for us to make embryos?
14. What is semen analysis?
15. (If gay male couple): Can we make embryos from both of us?
16. Can we try for twins?
17. What are the risks of trying to have twins?
18. What do we do to find an egg donor?
19. Do you provide egg donors through your clinic?
20. If we cannot find an egg donor through your clinic, where do we look for one?
21. Can you give us recommendations of egg donation agencies?
22. What if the egg donor does not produce good eggs or enough eggs?
23. How can we minimize the risk to make sure we get an egg donor who will most likely produce enough eggs and good quality eggs?
24. How can we make sure that our surrogate is a good surrogate medically speaking and a good surrogate who will most likely get pregnant?
25. What are the success rates of getting pregnant on the first try at your clinic?
26. What are the success rates of getting pregnant in two or three embryo transfers?
27. How do we choose which embryo to transfer?
28. What happens during in vitro fertilization?
29. How many days do the embryos have to grow before they are ready to be transferred or to be frozen for embryo transfer later?

30. Will the embryos be frozen?
 31. What does it mean to do genetic testing on the embryos?
32. How is this done?
33. Can the testing of the embryos harm them?
34. What kinds of genetic test are done on us?
35. Is there genetic testing of the surrogate?
36. What kinds of genetic tests are done on the egg donor?
 37. How many times have you seen (or what is the percentage) that people need a second surrogate?
38. How many times have you seen (or what is the percentage), that people need a second egg donor?
39. When there is a pregnancy, do you keep treating the surrogate? For how long?
40. How does she choose an obstetrician? Do we have a say in that?
41. If the surrogate comes from a location not near your clinic, how does that work?
42. How many times does she have to travel to the clinic?
43. How is she monitored by you while she is on medication before the embryo transfer?
44. Can we be in contact with her during the time she is on medication and being monitored?
45. Can we come to the embryo transfer?
46. What are the fees and costs? Do you have an itemized breakdown?
47. Will our insurance cover any of the medical treatments?
48. What is the timing of the payments we must make to the clinic?
49. Will you be the one we speak to if we have questions? Will you be available to us? Will we have a case manager or case coordinator?
50. Do you have references of people we can talk to about working with your clinic?

When the intended parents narrow down the list of fertility clinics and agencies in which they are interested, they must then do a deeper dive into the details of the obligations and commitments that they must make to the clinic or agency, as well as the details of the obligations and commitments that the clinic or agency will make to them. This can be done by looking carefully at the onboarding documents and/or retainer agreements.

There are other questions that intended parents will have, and they may forget to cover some topics in their initial consultations. Another good sign from a professional is that he or she is willing to remain available to answer additional questions as they come up even if the intended parents are not yet signed on as clients.

When to Begin the Journey

There is no perfect time to begin a surrogacy journey. Every intended parent's journey is unique, and the path as well as the timing should be the right fit for the intended parents. There may be some specific reasons some parents turn to surrogacy at certain times.

Straight couples who have gone through fertility treatments (the intended mother has tried to become pregnant and perhaps has had numerous miscarriages or have endured other problems and losses) will turn to surrogacy because of their physician's advice or because they are weary. The intended parents are worn out and they decide that it is time to turn to surrogacy.

Intended parents must pay attention to these physical, psychological, and mental clues. It is so hard for such couples to turn to surrogacy because, of course, the intended mother desires to carry her own baby. But the intended parents have endured sadness and frustration. Together, they have weathered the storms of infertility, the emotions, the distress. The hope is that they have remained close and allied in their determination to have a child. This resilience will help them tremendously in their decision and efforts to turn to gestational surrogacy to have their children.

Some couples may be having trouble in their relationship because of the stress and strain of going through infertility. As Erica Berman, PhD, points out, "What most people don't realize is that infertility is a major life challenge for those involved. It causes distress and disruption to people's lives comparable to a cancer diagnosis, job loss, and divorce. It is not just about 'relaxing.' Infertility is often a medical problem requiring costly treatment. It can create a substantial financial burden for people; it can destroy a couple's intimacy; it can cause serious significant emotional distress and interfere with everyday functioning."[17] Intended parents who are suffering these types of stressors in their relationship should seriously consider seeking counseling. Relationships do not have to fray or end in separation or divorce due to the complications and stresses of infertility. Hardships can be overcome with a focus on the plan to have a family and on the love that brought the couple together in the first place. A further willingness to communicate and seek counseling, if necessary, may help the couple understand each other and find ways to make compromises and to stay in the positive light of their relationship. In fact, if couples can navigate these hardships together and if they decide to access counseling or couples' therapy, their relationships stand a very good chance of getting stronger.

The truth is that it will take work, but the effort is worth it. Couples that find themselves together on the other side of difficulties also find more intimacy, more love in their hearts for each other, and more empathy. As both partners move in this positive direction together, they will be able to communicate their needs and do better to lovingly meet each other's needs.

Same-sex couples must also decide when to begin their journeys through surrogacy. There is a myriad of decisions to be considered and made to start

---

17. Erica Berman, "When Infertility Affects Your Marriage," *Huffington Post,* January 23, 2014, retrieved December 3, 2020, https://www.huffingtonpost.ca/erica-berman/infertility-and depression_b_4251953.html.

the process. Although they do not usually have the years of infertility hardship, they most likely have something of a different issue, which is that they do not know a great deal about IVF, making embryos, testing embryos, embryo transfer, egg donation, and all the steps and details that go into a surrogacy journey. Without gathering information, the process may seem overwhelming and confusing, and they may not be aware of potential successes and frustrations they may encounter along the way. Unless they are physicians or medical providers who know a good deal about reproductive medicine, their need at first is to become informed. They come to the table with one simple goal, and that is to find a sound, stable, and good woman to carry their baby so that they can start their family, but the complexity and the potential complications of the process may elude them at first.

This deep dive into the world of surrogacy has its own set of stresses. For a same-sex couple, the intended parents must think about which one of them will become the biological father or the first biological father if they are planning two or more children. They may find that one intended father has sperm with good motility and the other does not. Will this create an issue in their relationship? They may want to try to conceive twins by using two embryos—one from the sperm of each intended father—but they will be facing the high risk of medical complications for both the surrogate and the babies in a twin or multiple pregnancy. If the original plan was to try to have twins, this thwarting of the original idea may lead to stress and frustration in the relationship.

All intended parents have questions, concerns, and fears about what the surrogacy process will be about, and if they will truly be successful at having a child in this way. Whatever obstacles come their way, it will be important for the intended parents to focus on solutions and gaining information to overcome the obstacles. It will be important to consult with competent professionals who can provide support, information, and encouragement if hardships are encountered.

Preparation is the key. Once the intended parents feel confident that they are emotionally and financially prepared to embark on their surrogacy journey to have a child, they will decide on their professional team and cross over from the planning stage to the actualization stage. This is a true milestone—a point in time when they make the commitment to themselves and to each other to realize their dream of having children.

How to Begin the Journey

Once the intended parents have made the firm decision to move forward, they must choose their professional team from the group of physicians and surrogacy agencies with whom they met. They must choose one fertility clinic and one surrogacy agency.

There is a process wherein intended parents do not use the services of a surrogacy agency, and this is when they independently match. While this will be discussed more fully in chapter 8, "What Is Independent Matching?" it means, briefly, that they have found a surrogate who is a friend or family member, or they have found a surrogate on their own without the matching services of the surrogacy agency.

Many medical clinics encourage or even require that intended parents utilize the support services of a matching agency even if they have independently matched with a surrogate. A reputable and experienced agency will provide screening of the surrogate, case management and support, surrogate support, supervision of legal processes, and overall supervision of the entire surrogacy process.

In terms of what to do first, there are variations. Some intended parents may choose their medical clinic first and go ahead with making embryos. If they need an egg donor, they will choose their egg donor through the medical clinic or an egg donation agency. Then they will work with their clinic to undergo the medical procedures to fertilize the eggs and create embryos. The embryos will most likely be genetically tested, and then they will be frozen until there is the match with the surrogate and the time arrives for the embryo transfer into the uterus of the surrogate.

Another model of initiating the surrogacy process is to choose the fertility clinic and the surrogacy agency at around the same time. Surrogacy matching programs almost always have a waiting period to be matched with a surrogate. These waiting times can range from approximately six to eighteen months or more. In fact, since the COVID-19 pandemic, the waiting times have increased. Intended parents should be careful of any agency promising a short waiting time. The common knowledge in the United States today is that there is an increasing demand for gestational surrogates. There are fewer surrogates for various reasons including whether they are vaccinated for COVID-19, and it takes at least a few months for the surrogate applicant to go through the screening including psychological evaluations, background checks, medical records review, and more. An agency promising a short matching time is probably not doing the prescreening of the surrogate. This is problematic for intended parents because it will set them up for a much greater chance of being frustrated and disappointed when a proposed surrogate candidate, with whom they think they are matched, does not pass screening.

During this waiting time, the intended parents will create their embryos. If they need one, they will look for and become matched with an egg donor. The medical procedures for the retrieval of the intended mother's eggs or the egg donor's eggs and the in vitro fertilization of these eggs will be done in the intended parents' chosen medical clinic. In this way, the intended parents are using the waiting time to their advantage to reduce the time it will ultimately take to have their baby.

The intended parents' main goal in terms of how to begin the surrogacy journey is to select the fertility clinic and the surrogacy agency. The only reason to not choose a surrogacy agency when initiating the surrogacy process is either because the intended parents have decided to create their embryos first and thereafter seek out their surrogate or because they have independently matched and the need for an agency is less likely.

Although independent matching will be discussed in chapter 8, "What Is Independent Matching?", it should be noted here that even when intended parents match independently with a gestational surrogate, there may still be a need to have a surrogacy agency on board. First, the fertility clinic may require it because the physician may want the parties to have the oversight and support that the agency will provide. Second, the intended parents themselves may desire the expertise, support, and coordination that the agency would provide. In these cases, the intended parents should explore whether an agency in which they are interested is available to modify its fee structure so that it may be retained to provide case management and/or surrogate screening without the component of matching the intended parents with a gestational surrogate.

At the fertility clinic, the intended parents will gain information about the clinic's surrogacy packages or plans and choose one. In general, the options may be as follows:

1. IVF with Surrogacy: This will cover semen analysis, storage of sperm, medical testing, medical procedures for egg retrieval, in vitro fertilization to create embryos, storage of embryos, and embryo transfers into the gestational carrier. In the event the first embryo transfer is unsuccessful, the clinical program will most likely include additional embryo transfers.

2. IVF with Egg Donation and Surrogacy: In this program, the same procedures as described in paragraph 1 above will be included, as well as an egg donor. The intended parents will choose an egg donor, who may be someone they know, or someone from an egg donation agency or the fertility clinic's egg donors. The egg donor will undergo the medical process to stimulate the production of her eggs, and she will undergo the egg retrieval procedure. Her eggs will be fertilized by in vitro fertilization. The resulting embryos will be stored and preserved until a surrogate undergoes the embryo transfer procedure.

The intended parents' first step at the clinic is to have a consultation with the reproductive physician to go over medical history and medical fertility needs. Some intended parents, such as heterosexual couples who have been experiencing infertility, may already have a relationship with a reproductive physician. Most likely, during their medical treatment for infertility, they will have this conversation about surrogacy with their doctor. Other intended parents, such as same-sex couples and single intended parents, may need to initiate contact with a reproductive medical clinic and engage in a first-time consultation.

After the consultation and if the intended parents decide to work with the clinic, they will have fertility testing. For a same-sex male couple or a single male, this testing will include a physical and semen analysis to look at sperm count and motility. For a straight couple, the male will have a semen analysis and the female will have a fertility work-up. There are also arrangements made by same-sex female couples who need to use a gestational surrogate. In such cases, the intended parents will work with their reproductive physician to determine a sperm source and whether they are able to use the eggs of one or both intended parents if they need an egg donor.

All women planning to become pregnant, whether in a heterosexual couple, lesbian, or single, will undergo a fertility work-up. This will include pre-conception screening labs and blood work to check for iron deficiency, sexually transmitted diseases, and checking for diabetes. The screening may also include a sonogram to look for any uterine issues (polyps, endometriosis, scar tissue) and an ultrasound to look at uterine volume and ovarian reserve. Often, genetic screening is also conducted.

The next step will be embryo creation unless embryos have already been created and are frozen in storage. Same-sex male couples will need an egg donor, so they will need to choose a donor from the clinic or work with an egg donation agency or egg bank. Or they may have a known donor who is a friend or a relative. Same-sex female couples will need a sperm donor. Similarly, they will need to choose a donor from a sperm bank, or they may have a known donor who is a friend, acquaintance, or relative. Heterosexual couples may be using their own egg and sperm, or they may also seek to utilize gametes from an egg and/or sperm donor.

An egg donor's cycle is about three weeks long. After egg retrieval, the clinics usually use intracytoplasmic sperm injection (ICSI), whereby sperm is injected directly into each egg. This process will be explained to intended parents in much greater detail when they have their consultations with their reproductive physicians.

Often, with same-sex male couples, they divide the eggs and inseminate half of the eggs with the sperm of one intended father and the other half with the sperm of the other intended father. From there, the embryos are grown in the lab. The intended parents will usually get an update each day letting them know how the embryos look and how they are developing.

The hope is that the embryos will grow for five days, when they will then be at the blastocyst (a rapidly dividing ball of cells) stage. Some embryos will stop growing before they get to this stage. When the embryos are at the blastocyte stage, most clinics will biopsy the embryo and send it out for preimplantation genetic screening (PGS) testing. Once biopsied, the embryos will be cryogenically frozen, placed in straws, labeled, and stored. The PGS test results take a couple of weeks. There will then be a report as to how many of the embryos are normal. There will also be a call or appointment to review these results with the doctor.

Heterosexual couples may have a similar process of creating and testing embryos. They may attempt to create embryos using the eggs of the intended mother. If this is not possible, the intended parents will decide if they will use an egg donor for embryo creation. Either the intended mother or the egg donor will start medication that will stimulate her ovaries to produce multiple mature eggs. Once medication begins, she will have appointments every two or three days to check on the egg count and the hormone levels in her blood. It will take from ten to fourteen days for the eggs to mature. When there is an ultrasound that shows a high number of mature eggs, she will receive a trigger injection to release eggs. Then, an egg retrieval will be scheduled two to three days later. There will be an ultrasound to help guide the doctor with a needle to remove the eggs from the ovaries. The procedure takes fifteen to thirty minutes and there will be a recovery period after the procedure.

If the intended parents are planning to use a gestational surrogate, and the intended parents have been matched with a prescreened surrogate, the first step at the medical clinic for the surrogate is the medical screening appointment. At this appointment, she will undergo a sonogram (a minimally invasive ultrasound technique that provides pictures of the inside of a woman's uterus), blood work, urinalysis, and a medication review. She will have a consultation with the doctor and possibly a psychological screening and group visit with the intended parents. This will be facilitated by a psychologist, or a mental health provider experienced in surrogacy counseling. The results from these screening procedures will be available in approximately two weeks and, after that, if the screening has gone well, the IVF clinic will work with the gestational surrogate for her to commence medication to prepare her uterine lining for the embryo transfer, and the embryo transfer date will be planned.

The gestational surrogate will be provided with medications and will be instructed to start them on a certain day. Prior to the medication start, she will have a baseline ultrasound and bloodwork. Then she will begin taking estrogen and, possibly, another medication called Lupron. About a week prior to the embryo transfer, she will have a uterine lining check. The physician will check to see if the uterine lining is developing to a certain thickness. The physician will look for some other factors of readiness and will prescribe orders for bloodwork to check the gestational carrier's hormone levels.

Three days prior to the embryo transfer, the gestational surrogate will start another hormone called progesterone. This is a hormone that helps prepare the gestational carrier's uterus for the implantation of a fertilized egg and helps to maintain a pregnancy. On the embryo transfer day, the gestational surrogate will have an ultrasound to check her uterus just before the transfer.

Prior to the embryo transfer, the intended parents' frozen embryo will be thawed and placed into a catheter (a thin, flexible tube used to transfer the embryo into the uterus). The catheter is then inserted into the uterus of the surrogate, and the embryo is placed in the uterine lining. The surrogate will rest for about a half hour and then can head home or back to the hotel. Each clinic has a different protocol although they are similar. Some may require bed rest or modified bed rest, while others instruct the surrogate to simply take it easy.

To determine whether there is a pregnancy, the surrogate will have bloodwork done approximately two weeks after the embryo transfer, depending on the clinical protocol as determined by the treating IVF physician. If the bloodwork confirms a pregnancy, there will be an ultrasound a couple of weeks later to check on embryo development. After another two weeks, a second ultrasound will be performed to check for a fetal heart rate. Medications, under the supervision of the IVF physician, will continue for ten to twelve weeks of pregnancy.

Once the intended parents choose their surrogacy agency, they will become familiar with the agency's retainer agreement if they have not already done so. This is the contract between the intended parents and the agency. It is the document that sets forth the obligations of the agency to the intended parents, as well as the obligations and commitment of the intended parents to the agency. The most basic obligation is the payment structure. There most likely will be an initial deposit, and then the remainder of the agency fees will be due according to the agency's timeline for payment of fees, although agencies vary in their payment expectations and, therefore, the intended parents should familiarize themselves with the payment structure and obligations.

The scope of the work that the agency says it will perform should be clearly set forth in the retainer agreement. The retainer agreement will state that the agency will match the intended parents with a gestational surrogate. This should be set forth in more specificity, for example, that the agency will match the intended parents with a qualified, screened surrogate. In this light, the agency should also set forth what is included in the screening of surrogate applicants. Screening should include a full psychological evaluation and a full background investigation. If the surrogate is married, her spouse will also undergo the psychological and background screening. Further, evaluation of a surrogate candidate should include a home visit by a social worker or a private investigator. The surrogate must be medically cleared by the intended parents' chosen reproductive physician. Every gestational surrogate candidate must be thoroughly and rigorously screened. This screening protocol should be set forth in the retainer agreement so that the agency contractually obligates itself to conducting and coordinating the screening of the surrogate.

The retainer agreement should address what happens if a surrogate does not work out and the match must be broken. First, how often does this happen and what are the reasons it might happen. These matters should be discussed with the intended parents. Then the following questions should be answered: Will the agency provide another surrogate? Is there a fee for this? What is the approximate waiting time for a second surrogate? Do the intended parents go to the end of the waiting list or are they prioritized?

The retainer agreement should also include provisions for having a second child with the same surrogate, or embarking on a second journey, also known as a sibling journey, or a second journey with a different surrogate and the related agency fees for these subsequent arrangements.

The retainer agreement is a contract between the surrogacy agency and the intended parents. It should be readable and understandable. Most importantly, if the intended parents have questions about the retainer agreement, or if there are provisions in it that they do not fully understand, they should make these questions and concerns known to the agency, and they should be able to get satisfactory answers to their questions. Taking it a step further, if the intended parents feel they should have a lawyer review the retainer agreement on their behalf, they should take the step to obtain independent legal counsel to provide them with advice and explanation about the retainer agreement. The intended parents may waive the option to obtain independent legal counsel to review the agency retainer, but they should know that this is an option for them. If they are inclined to seek such legal counsel, they should hire a lawyer who has experience in surrogacy and reproductive law.

Once the intended parents choose a plan with their fertility clinic and make a deposit to the clinic, they have begun the IVF process. Once they execute the retainer agreement with the surrogacy agency, they have become clients of the agency, and the agency should immediately begin its work on their behalf.

Along with the retainer agreement, the intended parents will also complete a profile for the agency to use in the process of matching them with a surrogate. The profile will include personal information, including an essay or story that the intended parents will write about themselves that will be shared with prospective surrogate candidates. This may cover the story of their relationship and how they got together; what they love about each other; things they like to do such as travel, sports, and hobbies; and what brought them to surrogacy: their desire to have children, their fertility hardships, or simply that they are a gay couple and looking for a special someone to carry their baby. The profile will include photos of, for example, their wedding, vacations, and happy times with extended family.

To summarize, the intended parents will officially start their surrogacy journey when they choose their fertility clinic and make a payment toward the medical procedures to be undertaken there and when they retain their surrogacy agency, make their first payment, and complete their intended parents' profile.

5

Who Becomes a Gestational Surrogate?

There are women in the world who are very passionate about children, family, pregnancy, and giving birth. They are wonderful mothers to their own children. They are happy in their families whether they are married or not. These are the women who become gestational surrogates. Of course, there is more to it than this, but these are the starting points.

In one way or another, the idea of becoming a surrogate has touched their lives. There are various reasons this has come about. The women who become surrogates are very fertile, they have had a very easy time of becoming pregnant, and the births and deliveries of their children have gone well. They value pregnancy and birth as well as the fact that pregnancy and birth have come naturally for them. Often, they have become aware of the struggles of infertility through a friend or family member or through stories in the news and on other media. This moves them to want to help to create a family. They may become compassionate or altruistic surrogates by helping a friend or family member and declining compensation. In the alternative, they may decide to apply to become a surrogate through a surrogacy agency. In this way, they will receive compensation and reimbursements for their services as a gestational surrogate. They may also find a match independently without an agency, and they may receive compensation and reimbursements for such an independent match.

Sometimes, women become aware of gestational surrogacy through friends or family members who have become surrogates. They see this as a possibility for themselves since they know that pregnancy and birth come naturally and easily for them. They then explore the possibility by talking to other women who have become surrogates or by researching surrogacy and inquiring about it with surrogacy professionals and with team members of surrogacy agencies. Many reproductive clinics and surrogacy agencies have women on their teams who were gestational surrogates, and these former surrogates provide a wealth of relevant information for potential surrogates.

It is important and necessary for women who desire to become surrogates to speak to experienced surrogates. More than the professionals such as lawyers and physicians, the experienced surrogates can convey the practical and emotional experiences of becoming a surrogate. The experienced surrogates can offer advice and information about what the screening process is like; what the medications are, how they are administered, and what this is like physically; and how to consider and decide on which parents they will carry a baby for. Experienced surrogates can share experiences about relating and communicating with intended parents. They can describe firsthand experiences of what it is like to give birth to a baby that will not be theirs to raise, to give the baby to the intended parents, to see the joy on the faces of the intended parents. They can also describe the hardships that may be encountered, such as failed embryo transfers or miscarriages.

Much of the practical, medical, and legal information about surrogacy will be and should be explained by the physicians and lawyers, as well as other surrogacy professionals and providers. Still, the sharing of experiences by surrogates who have gone through surrogacy journeys is a treasure trove for women considering becoming surrogates.

Many intended parents are concerned that they will be taken advantage of. After all, how much more vulnerable could they ever be than to hope and trust that another human being will go through fertility treatments and pregnancy to bring their baby into the world? One common concern is that the surrogate will want to keep the baby. In gestational surrogacy, under the proper professional supervision and with the rigorous screening of surrogate applicants, these two concerns will not materialize. There are cases that can be found on the Internet and elsewhere about surrogacy arrangements that have not gone well, or relationships between intended parents and surrogates that have broken down. These cases were most likely not handled by an experienced and reputable team of professionals. They are cases of independent matches or matches handled by incompetent and inexperienced people trying to make surrogacy matches. In these cases, it is likely that rigorous and careful screening was not done at all or at least not thoroughly enough to significantly reduce such risk.

The women who successfully go through screening and become surrogates do not want to take advantage of anyone. They want to help bring a baby into the world to foster joy and to bring the gift of a baby to the intended parents. If they want to have a baby, they will have their own baby. Since they do not want to have any parental or financial obligations for the infant, they want to be sure the intended parents will take responsibility for the baby and meet their obligations in the surrogacy agreement. Surrogates also expect the intended parents to attend the birth so they can immediately assume responsibility for their baby.

It is important to understand that women who become surrogates do so because they want to help to bring a baby into the world and to create a family for the intended parents. Women who become surrogates are relational. They want to have connections with their intended parents. They are not doing this just for the money. It is an intimate and profound experience for surrogates and intended parents to come together and be there for each other throughout the pre-pregnancy, embryo transfer, pregnancy, delivery, birth, and post-partum aspects of the surrogacy journey.

Women who are compensated as gestational surrogates are looking at the endeavor as something they are capable of, something they can contribute to the world and lives of their intended parents. While the money is important and will help them and their families, it is by far not the only motivating factor. The women who become surrogates are compassionate, loving women who are healthy, sound, and stable. They view themselves as good at being pregnant and they want to share this ability to help intended parents have their children.

In fact, the money is most likely the secondary motivating factor for surrogates. Their primary motivation is to do something fulfilling and rewarding by helping the intended parents. Women who become surrogates have read about surrogacy and the various reasons intended parents turn to gestational surrogacy to have their children. They may know friends or relatives who have suffered through infertility or who cannot have children unless they have a baby through surrogacy. Surrogates believe and know that the children brought into these families will be loved and wanted children.

In their own words, here are some reasons women become gestational surrogates. The following is from N and her husband E:

We are N and E. We met and started dating while working at a small-town grocery store in 2007. N earned her associate degree in culinary arts management in 2010 from the Culinary Institute of America in New York, and E enlisted in the Army Reserves from 2008 to 2016. We married in 2013 and have two beautiful children. We currently reside in New Hampshire, where N manages the local senior center, which provides activities, resources, and Meals on Wheels for the community. E works at a local University. We enjoy any activity outdoors (hiking, camping, swimming), spending time with our families, who live close by, and working on our homestead, where we have a dog, multiple fish, chickens, and an enormous vegetable garden. Our journey as parents has taught us so much about ourselves, our marriage, and the true meaning of family, and we would love to be able to help others experience the joy that having children brings. We can promise you, there are no easy days, and sometimes you may want to pull your hair out! But, at the end of each night when you are watching your little one dream sweet dreams, it makes all the difficult moments of the day worthwhile. We can't wait to be part of this journey with you.

The following are additional remarks from women who have become gestational surrogates.

AA: Becoming a mother has been the greatest journey in my life, and I would love to provide the joy and unconditional love a child brings to a family who cannot do so on their own.

SA: I was adopted by my parents, who struggled with infertility, and surrogacy wasn't really an option then. I enjoy being pregnant. To help a family have what I have is the best feeling.

JB: Having seen firsthand how beautiful surrogacy can be, I couldn't imagine not doing this again! Helping a couple achieve their dreams of parenthood is truly something special. I can honestly say that, aside from having my own children, being a surrogate has been one of the most rewarding moments of my life.

CD: When having my son changed my life for the better, the idea of giving that to another family is an easy decision. Everyone deserves to have a family of their own.

AE: After getting that rewarding feeling from completing my first journey, I knew for a fact I wanted to do this again for another family. Surrogacy is near and dear to my heart, and I would love to continue to help families grow.

ME: I feel deep empathy for women who are not able to conceive and carry to full-term. I have several friends who have struggled with infertility and/or miscarriages, and it breaks my heart watching them struggle. I feel called to help someone who has had similar struggles and to carry their baby for them.

HF: I genuinely loved being pregnant and had very smooth pregnancies. I would love to help someone who may be unable to maintain a pregnancy or who is struggling with infertility.

CG: Being a surrogate has brought joy to the families I have been honored to serve. I am healthy enough to do it once more! Being called to be a surrogate has been a very rewarding experience, and I have been so blessed to be such a part of the lives of these parents and babies.

TH: It has always been my dream to be a surrogate, so I can give an individual the blessing of being a parent.

IH: My husband and I recently went through this process. We didn't expect it to be so rewarding. Seeing the new parents hold their baby for the first time was the most beautiful thing for my husband and me to see. Throughout the pregnancy, I ate healthier and exercised, knowing I was carrying someone else's baby. It was the easiest pregnancy I've had yet—a perfect delivery and a healthy baby girl.

NK: I think I'd be a great surrogate. I am young and healthy and loved being pregnant. I'm aware of the risks involved, but I choose to look at the result: helping a couple or individual have the gift of a child.

DL: I've wanted to be a surrogate since I was nineteen. I can remember interning at a law firm and hearing a paralegal talk about how her friends couldn't have kids. I knew instantly I could do that! I went to research the possibility, only to discover I was unable to since I did not yet have my own children. A few years later I became a mother, and I researched the idea again. I was able to meet the Worldwide Surrogacy team and start my journey. I've been so thankful to meet a great couple and help them complete their family. I love the warm feeling I receive helping others. I volunteer often, and being a surrogate is just another way for me to help someone else in need. To help a family complete their family is a great honor that I can accomplish.

SM: In a nutshell, being a surrogate has been such a wonderful experience, and I think after such a tough year for everyone across the globe in 2020, I want to do something positive and good for someone else in the beginning of this new year.

CM: Everyone who wants a child should have the opportunity to no matter how they are born. When I was younger, my parents wanted to have another child, and they were not able to. When I was older and my parents told me this, it gave me the longing in my heart to help someone have their miracle baby. Having and loving my own children gave me even more drive to want to help someone experience life's wonderful miracle of a baby. And then I became a surrogate. Nothing can describe the feeling when you give birth to a baby and see the baby in the arms of the parents who have been praying for this baby. It's an amazing and humbling experience!

SP: The first time around was amazing. I never thought the journey I took would impact my life so much. Seeing my last couple with their ever so gorgeous baby boy made everything so worth it (like the heartburn and swollen feet). I grew up with a very small family (pretty much just my mom and myself) and now have an extended family with the parents I carried for and their baby. There is nothing more rewarding.

MP: I enjoy being a surrogate because I know not everyone can have a family in a traditional way. I'm happy I can help. Seeing the parents' reaction of joy when they see and hold their child for the first time is a beautiful moment to witness.

SS: I have a soft spot for people with infertility. After having my two kids, I decided I wanted to help someone have a family, so I applied to be a surrogate. I thought I was a one-and-done surrogate, but I have been having the desire to do it again. It was such a rewarding experience, and I feel my body is ready to help one more family.

LS: I love being pregnant! But I do not want to have any more children of my own (my two kids are quite the handful!). Still, I love being able to give the gift of life and helping others any way I can.

JS: Nothing would give me greater joy than being able to be a part of such a miracle. I would love the opportunity to try and give a family the baby they've longed for.

JV: I enjoy pregnancy and it comes very easily for me. I have not had to endure any pregnancy-related complications, I have quick and easy deliveries, and I recover quite well. Surrogacy is a miraculous experience that has changed our lives. It would be an honor to help another family bring a baby into the world if I am able to do this again.

Where Do Surrogates Come From?

It does not matter where the surrogates come from in the United States if they come from a state where gestational surrogacy is legal, and, if the plan is to compensate the surrogate, then compensated gestational surrogacy must also be legal in the state.

Every state has its own set of laws, court precedents, and/or procedures for gestational surrogacy arrangements. The main concern in terms of location, for both surrogates and intended parents, is the law of the state where the surrogate resides because that is most likely where she will give birth. Most states are similar regarding the compensation standards for surrogates, although California is known to be a state where the surrogate compensation is higher than other places in the United States. The reason may be that many intended parents still think that California is legally the safest state for gestational surrogacy. While that may have been true many years ago, it is a myth now because many states have very clear laws and legal procedures in favor of compensated gestational surrogacy.

Surrogates also become educated about what their contracts and compensation packages may include. There are many online forums, chat rooms, and other resources of which surrogates may avail themselves to find out the financial standards and opportunities in compensated surrogacy. This is one reason there is a consistency in the United States in terms of the compensation packages sought by surrogates and accepted by intended parents. There is a range of compensation packages, but most fall within accepted standards and guidelines.

Intended parents must be matched with a gestational surrogate who lives in a state that is favorable—that is, where compensated gestational surrogacy is legal, where the gestational surrogacy agreement may be enforced, and, most importantly, where the intended parents are able to be named as the legal parents of their baby before the date of birth. Or if the birth is to take place in a state where there is a post-birth order of legal parentage, this must be available through a clear process ensuring that the intended parents will become the legal parents of their child very soon after the birth.

There are a myriad of different laws and procedures in the various US states that allow compensated surrogacy. When a match is proposed between intended parents and surrogates, the matching process must include informing the surrogate and intended parents on the law and process for establishing legal parentage. A competent lawyer should be available to advise the intended parents regarding the law in the state where their baby will be born.

Gestational surrogates come from all the states in the US, except for a few that continue to prohibit compensated gestational surrogacy. It is therefore imperative for legal counsel to weigh in on the location of a gestational surrogate in terms of the state law as it applies to the circumstances of the intended parents. For example, Louisiana and Michigan prohibit compensated surrogate. Texas and Utah require that the intended parents be legally married. Therefore, an unmarried couple must not be matched in the states of Texas or Utah. In Arizona, at least one intended parent must be genetically related to the baby being carried by the surrogate. Therefore, intended parents who use both an egg donor and a sperm donor to create their embryos must not be matched with a surrogate in Arizona. These are just a few examples demonstrating the need for competent, experienced legal counsel to be involved in the matching process.

This question of where surrogates come from is one asked by many intended parents because they want to know where their baby might be born, and if they will be legally safe in that state according to the laws and procedures for establishing legal parentage in a gestational surrogacy arrangement. In the case of intended parents who live in the United States, will the birth occur near where they live? Or will they have to travel a long distance to get to the place of birth? In the case of international intended parents, how far will they have to travel from their home country to arrive at the location of the birth? If they are from Europe, they may hope to be matched with a surrogate who resides on the East Coast of the United States, as this will be a shorter distance to travel to the place of birth. If they are coming from Asia, they may prefer the West Coast. These are some of the reasons location matters, and, therefore, the question of where surrogates come from is a common and legitimate question.

Intended parents will have their own perspective on the issue of the location of their surrogate. Many intended parents desire to be within driving distance of the residence of the surrogate, her obstetrician's office, and the hospital where the birth is planned to occur. In this way, they do not have to worry about getting on a plane or traveling a very long distance to get to the birth. In other cases, the intended parents may prioritize the time it takes to be matched, and so they will be open to locations that are not within driving distance. In this way, they will increase the pool of surrogates available to be matched with them. With this matching parameter opened, the intended parents may be matched more quickly than those that feel the need to wait for a surrogate near them.

Women who wish to become surrogates come from many different areas. Most live in suburbs and some in rural communities. There are few that come from urban areas. All live in reasonable proximity to good medical care and hospitals. They have had healthy pregnancies and uncomplicated births, having received medical treatment and good prenatal care in their own communities. This, too, is information that should be available to the intended parents when they are considering a match with a surrogate.

The Relationships between Surrogates and Intended Parents

Gestational surrogacy involves a group of people bringing a baby into the world. The group begins with the intended parents and their gestational surrogate. If she is married or has a partner, her spouse or partner are part of this group. Surrounding this group is the team of professionals and support people providing advice, legal and medical expertise, encouragement, compassion, attention, and support to the group.

It is practically inevitable that the surrogate and the intended parents become close and that they have a warm and positive relationship during the pre-pregnancy and pregnancy periods. They are coming together to join in one of life's most profound milestones, that is, to bring a newborn baby into the world through conception, pregnancy, and birth. Surrogates are motivated by experiencing the hope and happiness of the intended parents. If there are hardships, such as failed embryo transfers or miscarriages, the surrogates are motivated to get through these hardships together with the intended parents. And most of all, the surrogates are motivated by the joy in the moment that a newborn baby is placed in the arms of her or his parents.

There are rare times when surrogates and intended parents do not have very much communication. There was a case where the parents wanted to be anonymous from the surrogate. This was because they would be going back to their home country where surrogacy is illegal, and they did not want to have any mention of the surrogacy in their records to the extent they could avoid this. They felt that remaining anonymous from the surrogate would provide them with more security around the issue of having no mention of the surrogacy in their records or travel plans.

Whether or not this was a logical or plausible explanation of why the intended parents desired to remain anonymous is not something that should be judged. Intended parents come to the process with unique needs and desires, and, as long as the surrogacy arrangement can be managed in a way that all parties are respected and supported and in a way that the ethical practices are adhered to, then the intended parents may choose their respective parameters for their journeys. Of course, the surrogates have a choice as to whether such anonymity will work for them. The surrogate would know ahead of time about the anonymity request, so it would be an arrangement that she would enter knowingly and voluntarily. But such anonymity between parents and surrogates is unusual in the United States.

The reason for mentioning this case here is to further show that this was an arrangement that was difficult for the surrogate. As stated, the surrogates desire to have at least some connection with the intended parents. They are in it for the emotional fulfillment of giving birth to a baby and witnessing the life and family they are helping to create. In the case of the anonymous intended parents, it was crucial that the surrogacy agency team was in close connection with the surrogate so that she would get the support and recognition from the agency team even though she was not deriving this recognition from the intended parents.

Although the connection between the intended parents and the surrogate is deep and important, it is also true that many intended parents may desire to have their baby and move on from a close relationship with the surrogate. This does not mean that there is not a warm and positive connection during the pregnancy. And further, there is nothing wrong if the parents desire to let go of the relationship with the surrogate. The main thing is that the matching team at the surrogacy agency has done a very good job from the outset to match such intended parents with a surrogate who is informed that this may be what happens after the birth.

Also, in these situations, things can change. Intended parents may say at the outset that they are not sure if they want an ongoing relationship with their surrogate after the birth, but then they become close throughout the pregnancy, and they decide to remain in each other's lives. In one case, a straight couple from New York conceived twins with their surrogate in Texas. The babies were premature at birth, and the intended mother had to stay in Texas for six weeks while the babies were in the NICU. Fortunately, the babies did well, and they grew strong enough to travel home after six weeks. Although, originally, the intended mother was not sure if she would keep in contact with the surrogate after the birth of her babies, what happened was that while she was in Texas, her surrogate was the one person who was there for her and helping her to care for the premature twins. They became very close during this time in Texas and have remained close friends.

It is important that parents and surrogates remain open to how their relationships may evolve and grow during the crucial time of the pregnancy and birth. It is also important that parents and surrogates step out of themselves and into the shoes of the other. Everyone has needs during a surrogacy journey. The best journeys are fueled by appreciation, respect, good communication, and gratitude for each other.

Additional Medical Steps

The medical steps and procedures that a gestational surrogate may expect include:

1. a physical examination by her treating obstetrician who must provide medical clearance that she is healthy enough to undergo another pregnancy;

2. a psychological evaluation as part of the initial screening;

3. a physical examination by the intended parents' reproductive physician;

4. taking medications by injection to prepare the uterine lining for the embryo;

5. undergoing the embryo transfer (a medical procedure at the reproductive clinic where the physician uses a catheter to place the embryo into the uterus;

6. blood tests and ultrasounds for various purposes both pre-pregnancy and during the pregnancy; and

7. routine prenatal care during pregnancy.

Criteria to Become a Gestational Surrogate

When managed and supported by an experienced team of surrogacy profes-sionals, the journeys for both intended parents and surrogates go well. The process is not devoid of risk, but there are many risks that can be substan-tially minimized. One significant aspect of minimizing risk is the care taken to screen the women who apply to become gestational surrogates. The reason for the rigorous and thorough screening is not only to protect the intended parents and to minimize their risk but also to care for the surrogate applicants and to make sure they are healthy as well as physically and mentally prepared to become a gestational surrogate. The surrogacy arrangement and journey should be a positive experience for everyone, including the surrogate and her family. The recruiting and screening process is meant to set the stage and lay a foundation for these positive experiences and outcomes. See Chapter 7, section "Screening of Surrogates," for more detailed information on the quali-fications and requirements for women to become gestational surrogates.

Thoughts and Considerations for Gestational Surrogates

When a woman decides to offer to become a gestational surrogate, she is embarking on a journey that will become one of her life's profound milestones. The common milestones encountered in someone's life may include getting married or entering a committed relationship, giving birth, adopting a child, losing a loved one, landing a promotion or attaining an achievement in one's career, graduating or completing a course of study, or finishing a significant project such as writing a book. Surrogacy includes milestones for those involved, including the meeting of the surrogate with the intended parents, the embryo transfer, achieving a pregnancy, and ultimately, giving birth and creating a family for the intended parents.

Agreeing to become pregnant, carry a baby, and give birth for another individual or couple involves intimate connections and relationships that carry people forward in their lives. It is these intimate relationships that create the foundation leading to the milestone of bringing a newborn baby into the world. This is the first important consideration for surrogates: knowing that they will be entering into life-changing relationships, and that these connections are serious and significant for the surrogate and her family and for the intended parents.

Once a woman sees the gravity of the commitment to become a surrogate, she must consider the practical aspects of what it will mean in her life to become a gestational surrogate. How her family will manage the surrogacy is of paramount concern. Physical health and the risks of pregnancy must be considered. Most likely, the woman thinking of surrogacy is healthy and has had healthy, easy, and fulfilling pregnancies. She loves and values her children to such an extent that she wants to use her natural ability to have healthy pregnancies to help someone else have the joy of having a child. But she must also think about the facts that not all pregnancies are easy and healthy and that there is a risk in any pregnancy for complications. She must be aware of the risks and be willing to take the risk only after she has been fully informed—that is, by a reproductive physician. Pregnancy involves known risks, including miscarriage, gestational diabetes, preeclampsia, and loss of reproductive organs, and, to be clear, pregnancy does include a risk of death.

Some high-profile cases have served to inform women of the risks of pregnancy. "In June 2018, Serena Williams told *Vanity Fair* about her journey to motherhood, including the story of how she nearly died a few days after giving birth. . . . Beyoncé punctuated her *Vogue* cover with the story of how she developed a life-threatening pregnancy condition called preeclampsia, which can lead to seizures and stroke."[18]

Tahmesha Dickey died in childbirth. She was giving birth to her own baby. She was not a surrogate. The reason to illustrate this case is because she had a healthy, uneventful pregnancy with excellent prenatal care. "'Her pregnancy had been going well,' her husband said. 'She was not high risk and had been regularly going to her prenatal visits.' . . . Dickey died of an amniotic fluid embolism, an often-fatal complication in which amniotic fluid enters the women's blood stream. It occurs in 1 out of 10,000 pregnancies and doctors are unsure why it happens or how to prevent it."[19]

Although it is beyond difficult to hear the sad and devastating stories about complications in pregnancy leading to death, it is so important to face this for a number of reasons. One reason is so that the woman who wishes to become a surrogate is fully informed of the risk she is taking. Another reason is for the intended parents to realize what the surrogate is doing for them in taking this risk.

A woman thinking about becoming a surrogate must also think about her family. If she is married or has a partner, will she have the support of her spouse/partner? This is a very important aspect of moving ahead with surrogacy. The surrogate and her spouse or partner should be allied and aligned with embarking on the surrogacy journey. Although it is the woman who becomes pregnant, it is a family affair. Obviously, her spouse or partner is involved. There will be times when their sexual relationship is impacted. Further, her spouse or partner must be screened for sexually transmitted diseases and will have to enter and execute the gestational surrogacy agreement along with the surrogate.

Also, when a surrogate is married, the law says that her spouse is the presumed parent of any child she gives birth to. Therefore, her spouse will have to participate and be involved in the legal proceedings enabling the intended parents to become the legal parents of the baby that the surrogate carries and gives birth to.

---

18. Neel Shah, "A Soaring Maternal Mortality Rate: What Does It Mean for You?" Harvard Health Blog, https://www.health.harvard.edu/blog/a-soaring-maternal-mortality-rate-what-does-it-mean-for-you-2018101614914.

19. Erin Brady, Dr. Jennifer Ashton, Eamon McNiff, and Lauren Effron, "Dying to Deliver: The Race to Prevent Sudden Death of New Mothers," ABC News, May 16, 2018, https://abcnews.go.com/Health/dying-deliver-race-prevent-sudden-death-mothers/story?id=55015361.

If the surrogate candidate has children, and they are old enough to understand that she is carrying a baby to help create another family, will these older children be supportive, and will they want to participate in this endeavor that their mom is taking on? If she has younger children, what will be the impact on them? Will she be able to explain in positive terms why she is pregnant, having a baby, and giving this baby to another family? Has she considered how she will help her children to understand this hugely important aspect of the surrogacy process and outcome? Also, the surrogate should consider how being a surrogate may take her away from her family for short periods, such as traveling to the medical clinic and being hospitalized at the time of birth. Is there a support system in place to help her with her children and other responsibilities during these times?

The extended family should also be considered. If the surrogate has parents and siblings, will she tell them, and will she have their support? Is she self-conscious or fearful about what people will think, or does she have confidence about becoming a surrogate?

Most people rely on support systems in their lives: people who are there for them in good times and bad. A woman becoming a surrogate will consider the extent of her support system and whether this group of people in her life will be there for her during the surrogacy arrangement and pregnancy. Are they supportive? If the surrogate is close with extended family and/or has close friends in her life, it is important to seek and find positive attitudes from extended family and friends toward surrogacy to create a foundation for a positive and fulfilling journey for everyone involved.

The support system is even more important if the surrogate is not married or does not have a partner with whom she lives. In these cases, the woman will want to make sure that she has people and plans in place to help her with her children and her responsibilities, such as paying bills and managing the details of life during times when she is away, and especially in the event of a complication requiring hospitalization. Even if the surrogate is married or has a live-in partner, she should be asking herself who, in addition to her spouse/partner, comprises her support system. If she is unavailable, her spouse or partner may be busy with work, and may need additional help with their children.

Therefore, it is important for the woman seriously considering surrogacy to identify the people in her world who make up her support system. These people may be spouses or partners, parents or siblings, aunts, uncles, close friends, neighbors, or work colleagues. This consideration is for the protection and safety of the surrogate and for all involved to feel confident and secure in moving forward.

Along these lines, the surrogate should also look at her employment circumstances if she is working. It is important that her work environment will be conducive to and supportive of her involvement in a surrogacy journey. If she is reliant on her employment, there must be no concern that she would lose her job due to becoming a surrogate or because of a pregnancy. Even if such a threat or action amounted to employment discrimination, the last thing anyone would want is for the surrogate to lose her job and have an employment discrimination case on her hands. Even if it were a good case, this would be very far from ideal or favorable for the surrogate and her family, and it would not be a good turn of events for the intended parents or the surrogacy journey.

The surrogate candidate's social environment poses a similar concern. She should feel confident that she will be surrounded by a community that will be open to her becoming a surrogate. And if this is not the case, she must ask herself if she will have the resilience and fortitude to feel confident about being a surrogate even if some in her community do not look favorably upon her decision.

Medical treatment and health insurance are additional considerations. The surrogate should know that she may choose her medical treatment. There are some things she will be asked to accept, such as the intended parents' choice and location of fertility clinic, but during the matching process (see chapter 7, "The Work of the Surrogacy Agency," for details of the matching and screening process), she is entitled to find out about the clinic and the physicians before she agrees to a match. She does not have to accept a match if, for some reason, she is not happy with the choice or location of the intended parents' reproductive clinic.

Usually, the surrogate chooses her own obstetrician for medical treatment during the pregnancy, as well as the hospital where she will give birth. Also, though, the intended parents will want to know who these medical providers are, and they may have the ability through the gestational surrogacy contract to weigh in on these decisions. For example, most intended parents will want to make sure that the hospital will have a level 2 neonatal intensive care unit (NICU), and in these cases, the surrogate and the intended parents will work together to mutually agree on the hospital and, if necessary, the obstetrician. However, although the goal is for surrogates and intended parents to work together to decide on medical care, all parties must know that the surrogate is the patient, and she has the right to make decisions for her own medical treatment.

An opportunity presented to women who are considering becoming a gestational surrogate is to work with a reputable surrogacy agency. The alternative to working with an agency is to match independently. What are the differences?

To match independently means to find intended parents without the initial assistance of professionals such as agencies, doctors, or lawyers. The simplest example of this type of a match is when relatives help each other. For example, a woman will become a surrogate for her sister who has infertility conditions. Or a close friend will become the surrogate for the intended parents. These matches usually begin with an informal conversation and then, if the parents and their potential surrogate decide to take the next steps, they will see a reproductive physician to determine if the woman who is to become the surrogate is healthy and able to become a surrogate. This is done for her own health and safety as well as the potential for a pregnancy. Additional screening will be done to ensure the match is a good idea for everyone involved.

Some independent matches are made between people who do not know each other. They may find each other on the Internet or through mutual acquaintances. Matches such as these present risks that may not be adequately addressed if not supervised and managed by a team of knowledgeable professionals working at surrogacy agencies.

There are times when independent matches may work out fine, but there is a great deal of enhanced risk without the involvement of an experienced agency. In one such independent match, an intended parent embarked on a surrogacy journey with his good friend. He was a single intended father, and she was a married surrogate. The intended father and surrogate had been close friends for a very long time. At first everything was fine, and they were excited for the pregnancy. After she became pregnant, she incurred lost wages for certain medical appointments and other expenses such as unreimbursed medical bills. The intended father began to question the bills and to suggest that some of the lost time from work was not necessary and that some of the medical expenses were not pregnancy related. Eventually they were arguing over these matters, and they asked their respective lawyers for advice. The intended father became extremely stressed that she would not cooperate with the legal procedures to establish him as the legal parent. The gestational surrogate and her husband were distressed because she was pregnant and carrying his baby, and they felt that he was not honoring his contractual agreement with them. The baby was born, the intended father became the legal father, and the issues regarding the wages that were due were resolved, but the emotional damage could not be undone. People who were once best friends had a serious falling out and lost their friendship.

The problems can range from this kind of disruption of relationships to much more serious issues, such as a surrogate deciding that she will not terminate a pregnancy when the intended parents want to. In a 2013 case, a gestational surrogate, Crystal Kelley, became pregnant for a couple from abroad.[20] During the pregnancy, through an ultrasound, it was learned that the baby had a cleft palate, cyst in the brain, and multiple heart defects. The intended parents wanted to terminate the pregnancy and requested that the gestational surrogate undergo a termination of the pregnancy. The surrogate was concerned that she would lose her legal rights since she lived in Connecticut, where surrogacy contracts were enforceable at the time. She decided that she did not want to terminate the pregnancy, and she moved to Michigan, where surrogacy contracts were not enforceable. The surrogate gave birth to the baby, who did, in fact, have multiple serious medical conditions requiring numerous surgeries. The baby was placed for adoption with a couple that took in special-needs infants and children.

---

20. Elizabeth Cohen, "Surrogate Offered $10,000 to Abort Baby," CNN Health, https://www.cnn.com/2013/03/04/health/surrogacy-kelley-legal-battle/index.html.

The point of this case is to show that one of the most important issues in surrogacy is to reach an agreement about terminating a pregnancy in the event of a serious fetal abnormality would have been addressed. This is a critical factor in matching intended parents and gestational surrogates. Referring to this case is not for the purpose of determining who was right or wrong in the decision making regarding the baby that was born; it is for the purpose of emphasizing that intensive and rigorous screening can significantly minimize the risk of a case like this happening at all.

Why is it important for a woman to seriously consider that it will be best for her to work with a surrogacy agency? A good surrogacy agency is experienced and devoted to making sure that that all parties are protected, informed, and safe throughout the surrogacy journey. The American Society for Reproductive Medicine sets forth guidelines including advice and recommendations regarding the medical, legal, and ethical aspects of surrogacy.[21] The mainstream, reputable, and experienced surrogacy agencies follow these guidelines. The reason is to make sure that women who become surrogates and the intended parents with whom they are matched are advised, supported, and informed in this most intimate and complicated life-changing journey of bringing a baby into the world through gestational surrogacy.

For the surrogates, the agency will make sure that the surrogate is screened thoroughly, and while some may think that the screening is mainly for the intended parents' security, the screening is also to make sure the surrogate's health is safeguarded. If there is any risk to her health or life, she will not be able to become a surrogate. Again, this is for her safety. The agency will make sure that the surrogate receives fair compensation and legal protection by making sure that she has an independent attorney. The compensation package will meet the current standards of compensation for gestational surrogates in the United States. These standards vary slightly among the US states, but the experienced agency lawyers and representatives will know what amounts to the range of fair compensation. In addition, the agency will address the surrogate's views of what her compensation should be. Every woman who becomes a surrogate has a right to have input into what the terms of her compensation in her surrogacy contract will be.

There are many other benefits for the surrogate to work with an agency. The agency also screens the intended parents so the surrogate will be assured of being matched with good and stable intended parents. The surrogate will be supported. The agency will provide case management and support staff to keep in regular contact with her to see how she is doing, to make sure she is informed of the medical appointments and procedures, and to simply be a

---

21. Practice Committee of the American Society for Reproductive Medicine and Practice Committee of the Society for Assisted Reproductive Technology; American Society for Reproductive Medicine, "Recommendations for Practices Utilizing Gestational Carriers: A Committee Opinion," *Fertility and Sterility* 107, no. 2 (February 2017): e3–e10, https://www.sciencedirect.com/science/article/pii/S0015028216630054.

friend to her throughout the process. The agency staff will be in close contact with the IVF clinic and thereby create one foundational team (consisting of the medical clinic and the surrogacy agency) to assist the surrogate and the intended parents. Good clinics and good agencies keep in close contact with each other to maximize the potential for safety, security, and success of the journey.

Another very important item that the agency will oversee is the medical insurance for the surrogate. If a surrogate has medical insurance, the agency will make sure it is reviewed and that the health insurance plan will cover a surrogate pregnancy. Most women who become surrogates have their own health insurance, but many health insurance policies will not cover a surrogate pregnancy. Therefore, a professional review of the insurance is imperative. If the policy does not cover a surrogate pregnancy, the agency will work with insurance professionals to make sure that insurance for the pregnancy is obtained and that the surrogate will be insured.

This insurance oversight is critical because the surrogate will incur medical bills for her treatment. With a surrogacy agency as well as insurance professionals looking after the process, these bills will be monitored for payment. The expectation is that the bills will be covered by the health insurance, but if the bills are not paid through insurance, or if there are portions of the medical bills that are not reimbursed by insurance, the agency will manage these issues and follow through with the intended parents to pay the medical expenses that are not paid by insurance.

There is also the issue of the newborn's medical expenses. Usually, the intended parents put their baby on the health insurance plan they use to cover themselves. They notify their insurance company that they are expecting a baby and that they want to add their baby as a dependent on the health insurance plan. This is sometimes confusing in surrogacy because the medical providers may see the surrogate as the parent and assume that her insurance should be used to cover the baby.

Notably, in gestational surrogacy cases, the newborn's medical bills must be separated from the surrogate's account because the intended parents, not the surrogate, are responsible for the newborn's medical expenses. Hospitals must be apprised of this so that there is no confusion, and the surrogate does not have these additional medical expenses on her account. Someone must communicate this to the hospital where the birth will take place. In the hands of a competent surrogacy agency, this is another detail that will be managed by the agency team. The hospital billing department will be apprised to open a separate account for the newborn's medical expenses. The intended parents will provide their insurance information to the hospital to cover the baby's medical expenses.

The risk of confusion over these billing matters can be avoided when competent agency professionals or insurance professionals are monitoring and supervising the surrogacy journey and its insurance-related matters. This team will make sure there are escrow funds to pay bills and will follow through with making sure such bills are paid. The parents will receive accurate information on their baby's medical care and billing, and the surrogate will be protected from having any connection to or responsibility for the newborn's medical bills.

Other types of insurance will also be addressed. The surrogate will be covered with life insurance, and there may be coverage for disability. In the event disability insurance is not available, the agency will make sure that the surrogate's gestational surrogacy contract contains provisions for lost wages in the event she is placed on bed rest or work restriction, for recuperation periods after delivery, and for the missed time from work for medical and testing appointments. Further, the intended parents and the surrogate will be represented by attorneys in the drafting and negotiation of these terms so that all parties will have the ability to receive legal counsel. The lawyers will make sure that the agreement is fair and represents everyone's understanding regarding their rights and obligations.

The woman who desires to become a surrogate should have a good handle on the medical providers she would like to use for her medical care during the pregnancy and delivery. Usually, it is the obstetrician she used for the births of her own children as well as the hospital where she has previously given birth. If she has moved from the vicinity of these providers, she will want to investigate medical care she may access near where she currently resides. When she is approaching the match with the intended parents, she will be asked about the medical providers she will choose. Knowing ahead of time will add clarity to the process for her as well as for the intended parents. They may research the medical providers, and, if they have a concern, they will be able to discuss these concerns before the parties commit to the match. In this way, in the unlikely event they cannot come to a meeting of the minds about medical providers, the match will not go forward. This does not usually happen, but the point is that it will be better, and it will avoid later questions if the surrogate and the intended parents can investigate these matters ahead of formalizing the surrogacy match.

Finally, another very important consideration and requirement is that the surrogate have her own independent legal counsel. She will have a lawyer outside the surrogacy agency who will advise her as to the gestational surrogacy agreement, her rights and obligations, the compensation terms, laws, and legal procedures that will affect her during the surrogacy journey. See Chapter 7 "The Work of the Surrogacy Agency", Section f. "Case Management," for a discussion on the topic of the lawyer's independence/conflict of interest.

Every step of the journey is filled with details and a great deal of information that must be organized and attended to. The surrogate who applies to and works with the support and experience of a qualified and experienced surrogacy agency will be protected and supported as she navigates this complicated path. The following is a list of questions that surrogate applicants may consider asking the agencies with whom they are applying:

Agency Facts

How many deliveries do you have each year?
What type of support do you offer your surrogates?
Do you have meet-ups, online or in person, for your surrogates?
Are the meet-ups mandatory?
Will I have a case coordinator that I can reach to discuss concerns?
How many surrogates does each case manager work with?
Can I speak with former surrogates?
How long has your agency been in business?
How many employees does your agency have?
Will I be working with one person throughout my journey or different people?

Qualifications

Do you accept surrogates who do not want to terminate a pregnancy?
Can I start the process if I am still breastfeeding?
How long should I wait from the delivery of my own baby to become a sur-
  rogate?
What are the age requirements?
What is the BMI (body mass index) requirement?
What medical issues would disqualify me?
What pregnancy complications would disqualify me?
Can I be a surrogate if I am currently taking antianxiety or antidepression
  medication?
How many previous births are acceptable?
What is the limit on the number of C-sections?
Do I need to have had a baby of my own to be a surrogate?
Can I be on state assistance and be a surrogate?

Agency screening

How long does the screening process take?
What is involved in the screening process?
What is involved in the psychological screening?
What type of background check do you do?
What happens during a home visit?
How long does it take to get the results of my screenings?

Intended Parents

Where do most of your intended parents live?
How many intended parents are currently waiting to match with a surrogate?
Do you screen your intended parents?
Can I freely communicate with my intended parents after we match, or do we
  need to wait until contracts are signed?
Do you have mostly domestic or mostly international intended parents?
What type of communication are the intended parents looking for?

Matching

How does the matching process work?
How long does it take to match?
Do I need to finish screening before I can match?
If you send me a profile, do I have to accept those intended parents?
What happens after I match with intended parents?

Clinics/Medical

Where are the clinics that you work with located?
Will I have to travel? If so, how often and for how long?
What types of appointments are involved during the IVF cycle?
What medications will I need to take?
Will I need to give myself injections?
What are the side effects of the medications?
What happens during the embryo transfer?
Will I be responsible for any screening or testing costs?
Will I have to pay for my travel costs for medical screening and transfer?
Can someone travel with me?
How many days will I need to travel for medical screening and transfer?

Compensation

What is the base compensation?
What other things are compensated or reimbursed?
When does compensation start?
Are the standard fees negotiable for things such as a C-section fee?
If I deliver early, am I still compensated?
Do you have a higher base compensation for experienced surrogates?
If my insurance is surrogate friendly, will my base compensation be higher?

Legal

Can I choose my own attorney?
Can you recommend an attorney in my state?
Who do the intended parents use as their attorney?
Can I make changes to the contract with my attorney?
Will I need to go to court?
Will my name be on the birth certificate?
Does your agency require surrogates to sign an exclusivity agreement?
If I break the match after contracts are signed, will I be responsible for any
    repayments?
Do you issue a 1099? Will I have to pay taxes on the compensation I receive?

Escrow Account

Will there be a bank or escrow agency to hold funds?
How is it managed?

If agency does not hold escrow, what escrow agencies do you recommend to
   your intended parents?
How are escrow payments authorized?
How do you make sure that your intended parents have enough money in their
   escrow account?

Pumping Breast Milk

Do intended parents want the surrogate to breastfeed or pump after delivery?
Can I donate breast milk elsewhere if my intended parents do not need/want
   milk?
What is the typical compensation when pumping for an intended parent?

OB/Delivery

Can I have my own support person in the room for delivery?
Will the intended parents be in the room for delivery?
Will I have to be induced or have a scheduled C-section?
What happens if the intended parents don't make it to the hospital?
Do I have to deliver in a hospital?
Can I choose my obstetrician and delivery hospital?
Will the intended parents come to prenatal appointments and ultrasounds?

Insurance

Will my medical insurance cover the surrogacy?
Are there options available if I need insurance?
Are all medical expenses for prenatal care and delivery paid by the intended
   parents?
Further details on the screening, compensation, insurance, legal, medical, and
   independent-matching aspects of surrogacy are provided in the following
   chapters.

The Work of the Surrogacy Agency

Introduction

The work of a comprehensive, experienced, and reputable surrogacy agency is detailed, nuanced and complex. In general, the agency has two main functions: (1) to match intended parents with a screened surrogate and to consult with, advise, and provide case management support to the intended parents; and (2) to provide information to consult with, recruit, screen, and support gestational surrogates.

Consulting with and Advising Intended Parents

The initial work of the surrogacy agency with intended parents starts when they request a consultation. This meeting is a very important milestone for the intended parents and for the agency. It is the point in time when these parties begin getting to know each other. Often, intended parents interview several agencies to get an idea of where they will eventually place their trust. They should be prepared with questions and topics that they would like to go over with the agency representative. On the other hand, the agency representative must be prepared with information on the program, such as statistics, fees and costs, staff, the case management system, and surrogate recruiting and matching as well as a thorough synopsis of the surrogacy journey and how it will most likely unfold if the intended parents join the agency with whom they are consulting.

The agency should send one of its most informed and experienced members to the initial consultation, bearing in mind that the intended parents' need for clear and accurate information is paramount. The surrogacy agency hopefully does not see the meeting as a time to sell its service. In fact, if the intended parents are to believe and trust that this outfit will help them realize the dream of having a baby, they must talk with someone from the agency who listens to them and wants to know their story and who is compassionate about the need to turn to surrogacy, sensitive to the daunting costs that intended parents face, and knowledgeable and able to give up-to-date, clear, and concise information about the various aspects of gestational surrogacy in the United States.

During the consultation, the parents should be encouraged to ask questions and know that no question is too mundane, obvious, or intrusive. They will hopefully come away with good information as well as a resource they can turn to if they feel the need to follow up with additional questions or obtain more information. A good agency representative will want to have the opportunity to be a resource and to inform and help the intended parents along their way.

Recruiting Surrogates

One of the main responsibilities of the surrogacy agency is to recruit and screen qualified women to become gestational surrogates. The screening is crucial, as is the intensive agency work to find qualified, healthy women, because this screening and recruiting process protects the intended parents as well as the surrogate applicants.

Surrogate candidates are often disqualified because of conditions or complications they had during or after their pregnancies, such as gestational diabetes, preeclampsia, premature births, or postnatal depression. The physicians evaluating the surrogate's medical records have two goals: (1) they have an obligation to take every precaution that a woman who becomes pregnant in a surrogacy arrangement is not at undue risk of having her own health compromised; and (2) they want to maximize the chance of achieving a pregnancy and sustaining a healthy pregnancy for the intended parents.

There are many ways that agencies reach out to recruit surrogates although it does not really matter exactly how they do this, since what is important is that the applicants pass the screening assessments. Many agencies advertise both online and in print for surrogate applicants. Online advertising programs are done through Google, Facebook, Instagram, other social media platforms, and various surrogacy-related websites where ads are placed. Each applicant should go through a thorough and rigorous screening process, and only if she passes the screening will she be deemed qualified to be matched with intended parents.

Word of mouth is another important method to recruit surrogates. An agency that has been matching parents with surrogates for years will have numerous surrogates that they have worked with. If the surrogates' experiences were good with the agency, they will most likely refer friends and family members who may want to become surrogates to the same agency. Some agencies may be proactive and offer their surrogates a commission to refer a qualified surrogate. This networking is very effective because women who have been surrogates are better able to describe what surrogacy is about, what it entails, and what it has been like for them to be a surrogate for a family.

There are also websites which have classified pages for surrogates and intended parents. Here, people can place information about themselves and look for a match. This will be discussed in chapter 8, where the topic of independent matching is covered. On some of these websites, agencies may also present nonidentifying profiles of their intended parents to see if there are any surrogates reviewing the site who may be interested in these intended parents as a suitable match.

The agency will have a team of people to handle the recruiting process. Each surrogate applicant will be greeted by someone from the agency after the initial application is submitted. If the surrogate meets the preliminary criteria (described below), she will be supported and assisted as she enters the more intensive screening assessments, such as the psychological evaluation and background investigation. The important aspect of the agency's work is that the agency team keeps in close communication with the surrogate applicant as they assist her in the screening process. In this way, two important goals are achieved: (1) the surrogate begins to feel that she is supported, respected, and appreciated; and (2) the agency team is getting to know the applicant, and, in this way, they may assess what her needs and strengths are in becoming a surrogate.

For example, some surrogates are independent and do not seek very much communication from the agency support team, while some surrogates greatly enjoy chatting and asking questions with the agency support team. A good agency will have a team that focuses on each surrogate as an individual and assists her accordingly.

Screening of Surrogates

For intended parents to place their trust in a woman they do not yet know to carry their embryo and gestate the embryo until she gives birth to the intended parents' baby, they must feel as completely secure and confident in the surrogate as reasonably possible. The foundation that leads to this trust and confidence is the screening that surrogate applicants must undergo. The surrogacy agency will coordinate this screening together with the fertility clinic.

Experienced and reputable surrogacy agencies will have similar screening protocols to follow certain standards that have emerged in the world of fertility treatment and gestational surrogacy. First, there are the preliminary requirements. These include the following.

1. The surrogate applicant must have given birth to her own children.
2. She must live in a US state that is legally favorable for gestational surrogacy.
3. All her births must have been healthy, full-term, and without complications such as gestational diabetes, preeclampsia, or other pregnancy-related conditions.
4. She must be between the ages of twenty-one and forty (occasionally a surrogate is approved if she is over forty, but this would be an exception that a reproductive physician would determine).
5. Her BMI (body mass index) must be within a range acceptable to the parents' reproductive physician (the medical clinics have clear standards).

6. She must not be on any prescribed medication.

7. She must not be on welfare or Medicaid. (This is for the benefit of the surrogate because she will be at risk of losing these benefits if she receives compensation as a gestational surrogate.)

Once the surrogate meets these preliminary criteria, the agency will work in coordination with the fertility clinic and require the surrogate applicant to go through the following additional screening:

1. A psychological evaluation by a licensed clinical psychologist (if she is married, her spouse will also be evaluated by the psychologist).

2. The MMPI or PAI administered by the psychologist conducting the psychological evaluation.

3. A background investigation by a licensed private investigation firm (if she is married, her spouse's background will also be subject to the investigation).

4. A home visit or home check by a social worker experienced in doing home studies or by the private investigation firm.

5. An examination for medical clearance from the applicant's obstetrician.

6. All the surrogate's pregnancy-related medical records will be submitted to the IVF physician for review and approval; and

7. A physical examination by the IVF physician and blood tests for the surrogate and her spouse for further screening and analysis.

The psychological evaluation should be done by a licensed clinical psychologist, and if the applicant is married, her spouse will also be evaluated by the psychologist. The surrogate will also take a standardized personality test, either the PAI (Personality Assessment Inventory)[22] or the MMPI (the Minnesota Multiphasic Personality Inventory).[23] The test will be scored and interpreted by the psychologist doing the evaluation.

A background investigation will also be done. This should be a comprehensive background check carried out by a licensed private investigation firm.

---

22. The Personality Assessment Inventory (PAI), "authored by Leslie Morey, PhD, is a multiscale test of psychological functioning that assesses constructs relevant to personality and psychopathology evaluation (e.g., depression, anxiety, aggression) in various contexts, including psychotherapy, crisis/evaluation, forensic, personnel selection, pain/medical, and child custody assessment," https://psychology.wikia.org/wiki/Personality_Assessment_Inventory.

23. The Minnesota Multiphasic Personality Inventory (MMPI) is a standardized psychometric test of adult personality and psychopathology. Psychologists and other mental health professionals use various versions of the MMPI to help develop treatment plans, assist with differential diagnosis, help answer legal questions (forensic psychology), and screen job candidates during the personnel selection process or as part of a therapeutic assessment procedure. The original MMPI was developed by Starke R. Hathaway and J. C. McKinley, faculty of the University of Minnesota, and first published by the University of Minnesota Press in 1943. It was replaced by an updated version, the MMPI-2, in 1989; see https://en.wikipedia.org/wiki/Minnesota_Multiphasic_Personality_Inventory.

A good investigation will include checking for any criminal history, including felonies, misdemeanors, and even traffic infractions. It will also include prior residence history for a period of at least ten years (with this information, the stability or reliability of the applicant can be assessed); civil court lawsuits, including debt collection cases; phone numbers; bankruptcy records; drivers' licenses; firearm permits or ownership; car and voter registration; neighborhood profile; property ownership records; and a list of residents in the household. Additional background investigations will be done on all adults living in the home of the surrogate applicant. There will be a home visit or home check, and this will include photos of the home and neighborhood.

There will be medical screening. The surrogate candidate will first go to her own obstetrician to obtain a letter of medical clearance. In addition to this, the surrogate applicant's pregnancy medical records will be obtained. To ensure that a complete and accurate set of records is obtained, the screening team must get these records from the actual medical providers and not from the surrogate applicant herself. These will be given to the reproductive clinic for the fertility physician's review. If the physician reviews the records and makes a finding that the surrogate may be approved to continue as a surrogate, she will then be eligible to be presented to intended parents who may be interested in her profile. The surrogate applicant is also given profiles of intended parents as she may also choose the parents with whom she wishes to be matched.

At this point, one action has yet to be taken—that is, the physical examination of the surrogate by the reproductive physician. Usually, that happens after the match is confirmed and the parties have entered a gestational surrogacy contract. The reason for this is so that legal clearance (verified by the existence of a fully executed gestational surrogacy agreement) should be provided to the IVF clinic before the surrogate visits the clinic and becomes the clinic's patient.

There are alternatives to this model. In some cases, the physical examination of the surrogate by the reproductive physician may be done before the gestational surrogacy contract is done. In this way, the gestational surrogate is medically screened prior to the parties entering a gestational surrogacy contract.

Either process is acceptable, and what is most important is that the intended parents and the gestational surrogate are aware of the process, and they know the order of the procedures, such as the review of records, entering into the surrogacy agreement, the surrogate's schedule of clinic visits, and other processes. Many clinics and surrogacy agencies have similar processes, but there may be variations. For example, at some clinics, they have what is called the marathon day. This is a day when the surrogate, her spouse or partner (if she is in a committed relationship), and the intended parents meet at the clinic and attend sessions alone and together with the clinic's counselor and the reproductive physician. By the time this occurs, the parties know each other very well and the agency screening has been done, so, most likely, this day of sessions is more informative and a way to get to know each other better.

But there are times when problems may arise during this day of meetings at the clinic, as, for example, when a transgender intended parent engaged in her first potential match with a surrogate. At that meeting in the clinic, the surrogate's spouse expressed concern that his wife would be carrying for a transgender intended parent. This led to the breakdown of this proposed match. This was a disappointing and frustrating outcome, but thankfully, the agency and clinical team went to work immediately to find a wonderful, positive surrogate for the transgender intended parent, and the parent was able to fulfill her dream of having a baby.

In another case, the intended parents learned on the marathon day that the surrogate was not willing to terminate the pregnancy if the fetus had Down's syndrome. The intended parents could not accept this and wanted to make sure they would have the ability to request a termination under any circumstances. The match broke down, and the parents had to be matched with a different surrogate.

These are rare exceptions on marathon days. Usually, people are happy to meet, they are already on the same page with these important concerns, and the match proceeds. However, even though the above-described cases sound devastating, disheartening, and even politically incorrect, it is best for all concerned that the issues come out in such clinical settings before more medical procedures are undertaken, such as an embryo transfer, and especially before pregnancy.

If the surrogate applicant does not complete or pass any one of these tests or evaluations, she will not be approved as a surrogate. Only approximately 3 percent to 5 percent of women who apply to become surrogates make it through the screening and are deemed qualified. While this creates a demand for surrogates and a waiting time for intended parents, it is a good thing. Such thorough screening will set the stage for a surrogacy that has stability and security for all of the parties, including the important intangible aspects of the journey, such as a good relationship between the surrogate and the intended parents; a surrogate who will be dedicated, committed, and compliant with her obligations to fulfill this commitment; and a positive and authentic foundation to bring the intended parents' baby into the world.

This screening protocol should be described and explained to the surrogate applicants, so they are prepared to undergo all examinations during the process. It should also be described to the intended parents, so they know how the agency is screening the surrogates. Usually, intended parents ask about the screening, but occasionally they do not. The description and explanation of the screening process will add a level of confidence and assurance to the intended parents. All intended parents are concerned about the idea that someone they do not know will be pregnant with their baby and, therefore, even if they do not ask about the specific screening protocol, telling them about it and providing them with a document detailing the screening protocol will greatly help to alleviate some of their natural concerns and worries.

Matching Intended Parents with Surrogates

In a well-run surrogacy agency, the screening of the surrogate is done prior to the match being made. There are good reasons this must occur. Mainly, this will avoid disappointment and frustration for the parties. The surrogate, if she is screened before being matched, will have confidence that she is qualified to move ahead as a surrogate. The intended parents will also have confidence, and they can now get to know their surrogate without the anxiety that she may not work out as their surrogate. There is always some risk that the match will not work out, but the goal of the agency, in doing the screening before confirming the match, is to minimize the risk as much as possible. The matching process is not something that is done overnight or quickly. Great care and attention to detail must go into it.

The matching team will be aware of the profile details of their intended parents and surrogates. The team's work will focus on comparing profiles and eventually showing profiles to the intended parents. Before showing a profile to intended parents, the team will make sure that the surrogate candidate is interested in the parents. In this way, the possibility of parents favoring a surrogate profile but then finding out that the surrogate does not want to carry for them will be avoided. In hearing this, intended parents should not be concerned. All intended parents are matched if the criteria they have for a surrogate are reasonable. It is just that all parties have preferences. Some surrogates may want to carry for a gay couple and some for a straight couple. Some will prefer an intended parent couple, and some will gladly carry for a single intended parent. Many surrogates do not have such preferences, but it is the responsibility of the matching team to compare these factors and make sure they present appropriate and willing surrogates to the intended parents.

The intended parents and surrogates choose each other. Therefore, the agency work is important in the matching process. Behind the scenes, the agency is making preliminary matches that make sense and that will most likely work for everyone. When the matching team proposes a match to the intended parents, it has been well thought out, and it is a proposed match that will meet as closely as possible the needs and desires of the intended parents. Most importantly, the intended parents and the surrogate and her spouse, if married, are well advised and thoroughly informed about each other.

Case Management

Case management is a primary function of the surrogacy agency. It incorporates many aspects of support for the intended parents and their surrogate, and it will encompass the entire journey from the moment the intended parents choose to sign on with an agency until their baby is born and they are home from the hospital with the proper birth certificate. An agency should have team members who work on recruiting and screening surrogates, onboarding intended parents, and matching intended parents with surrogates and case managers. There should also be a legal department to provide information and supervision regarding legal matters throughout the journey. There may or may not be an escrow management system, but the agency will have knowledge about escrow management and provide resources and guidance about this aspect of the surrogacy journey.

The Case Manager

There will be a case manager who will be the main point of contact at the agency for the intended parents. As soon as the parents come on board with the agency, the onboarding team and/or the case manager will reach out and get to know them. She or he will review the profile completed and submitted by the intended parents and will assist the parents with completing their profile if the parents have questions or request assistance with completing it. The profile is the initial submission of information by the intended parents, and it is the main vehicle for the matching team and the case manager to begin to get to know the intended parents.

A good case manager will take time to carefully review the profile and to discuss it with the new intended parents. Her job at the outset is to get to know and understand the intended parents and, in this way, to better help them along the complex journey of gestational surrogacy as well as to set the stage to make the best match possible with a surrogate.

Parents often ask how many cases each case manager has. This is important information, but it must be reviewed in the context of the overall operations of the agency. A better question might be: How are cases allocated, and what is the system of case management? This will vary based on the management styles of the agency leaders. Some agencies may have a set number of cases per case manager. Some agencies may have a team approach, with a lead case manager taking on primary responsibilities, such as matching, and assistant case managers helping with administrative details as well as journey coordinators who provide support and case management as the match proceeds toward embryo transfer, pregnancy, and birth.

Also, the number of cases does not dictate the amount of work in surrogacy case management. Cases where the surrogate is pregnant are usually low maintenance for the case manager unless some medical problem or communication problem arises, and this is not common. If ten cases represent pregnancies, those cases will not be work intensive for the case manager providing the pregnancy is proceeding smoothly. The parents will have all the access they need to the medical records and condition of their surrogate, and the parties should be communicating well and enjoying the pregnancy.

Similarly, in cases that are in the hands of the clinic for the medical phase leading to the embryo transfer, the IVF clinic is more hands-on than the surrogacy agency. The case manager will know the details of the medical protocol such as the monitoring status, appointments, and embryo transfer dates, but the actual procedures and medical treatment will be scheduled by and performed at the IVF clinic.

The most active period for a case manager is during the actual matching of the intended parents and the surrogate when the parents are reviewing profiles, as well as when the surrogate is traveling to the IVF clinic for medical procedures such as starting medication and undergoing the embryo transfers. During the matching phase, the intended parents must be fully and thoroughly informed about each surrogate candidate they are considering. The case manager must be prepared with a great deal of information about the surrogate candidate. If the match is to be made, it will be possible only if the intended parents have answers to their questions about the surrogate, and if they develop confidence and security in choosing a candidate as their surrogate. In addition, the surrogate must be fully informed about the intended parents with whom she is considering matching.

Further, the case manager must be a liaison between the agency's surrogate recruiting and support team and the intended parents. The surrogate candidate, although already vetted about the proposed intended parents, may also have questions, and it is the job of the case manager in conjunction with the surrogate recruiting team to make sure that the surrogate is also well informed and develops confidence and security in the match.

Here are some comments and words of wisdom about what it means to be a case manager from some very experienced surrogacy agency case managers.

From Jennifer of Worldwide Surrogacy:[24]

1. *What do you like about being a case manager for parents going through surrogacy?*

I love watching the parents come in at the beginning with so many questions and so many concerns and fears of the unknown, and then watching the journey unfold to the first BETA[25] when they are pregnant. I love to help them along the way, from beginning to end with next steps, and it is incredibly fulfilling to give them ideas for how to work through things that concern them, to keep encouraging them if they are feeling discouraged or worried, and to just be their trusted friend and confidante in this most important part of their lives.

2. *What do you think are important qualities and skills for a good case manager?*

---

24. Worldwide Surrogacy Specialists, www.worldwidesurrogacy.org, 2150 Post Rd., Fairfield, CT 06824; (203) 255-9877.

25. A pregnancy blood test (quantitative beta-hCG) is more accurate than a urine pregnancy test. A pregnancy blood test may be used to verify whether or not a woman is pregnant, based on the hormones released by her body. This pregnancy test measures the blood level of beta hCG and is also known as the beta human chorionic gonadotropin (beta-hCG) test, https://www.labfinder.com/blood-test/pregnancy-blood-test-beta-hcg/#:~:text=Pregnancy%20Blood%20Test%20(Quantitative%20Beta,as%20Beta%20Human%20Chorionic%20Gonadotropin.

One of the most important qualities for a good case manager is to be a people person, to be friendly and especially to be understanding of the intended parents' situation when they initially come to us and to continue to be understanding as they proceed through their journey. Empathy is very important, to get into the shoes of the parents and let them know that you really care about what they are going through and how important it is that they are going through this to have their baby and create their family. It is also important to be flexible. People have their ups and downs, and at times the surrogacy journey will be stressful, so I think it is important to let them know we are working together as a team for the entire journey. There is a great deal of information that must be conveyed to and processed by the intended parents. Therefore, a good case manager must keep informed at all times, be organized, have good and clear communication skills, and be a good listener. Lastly, I think the case manager must be a good team player, as there are many moving parts and people to work with, from the medical clinical staff to the interoffice team and, of course, the intended parents and the surrogate.

3. *What are two or three things you would say to intended parents as advice to go through their surrogacy journey more easily and happily?*

I always tell people surrogacy is a wild but beautiful ride, and they should try to have a lot of trust and faith and patience when dealing with the system and the process. There will be disappointments, but that is why we are here: to help them stay on the path to having a baby.

The surrogates are human and have their own families and lives, and it's very important to be flexible and work together as a team. The best matches are the ones where each party has a mutual admiration/appreciation for one another, and this is not only about the intended parents having a baby but about the surrogate's experience as well.

From Jill of Simple Surrogacy:[26]

1. *What do you like about being a case manager for parents going through surrogacy?*

I think if you ask any gestational carrier, she will tell you that the best part of the journey is seeing the intended parents with their baby for the first time. It's a feeling that can never be recreated unless she does another journey. Obviously, there is a limit to how many journeys a surrogate can do. After four journeys of my own, I decided that I would still like to be part of the world of surrogacy. Although I am not the one giving birth, as a case manager, I still get to see the intended parents' joy and excitement

---

26. Simple Surrogacy, www.simplesurrogacy.com, 4925 Greenville Avenue, Suite 200, Dallas, TX 75206.

throughout the entire process. Getting to be part of each journey is a privilege and the next best thing to being a gestational carrier myself.

2. *What do you think are important qualities and skills for a good case manager?*

Good communication skills, patience, and compassion are the most important qualities for a case manager. This process is new to most intended parents, so it is important to keep them updated and explain each step throughout the entire process. As you can imagine, there are times when things don't go as planned or there are bumps in the road. It is important for a case manager to be available during those times, whether to talk things through and give reassurance or to just listen.

3. *What are two or three things you would say to intended parents as advice to go through their surrogacy journey more easily and happily?*

My biggest piece of advice would be to have patience. This is a marathon, not a sprint. I know every intended parent comes into a program ready to have a baby now. Most have been dreaming about this for years and are excited to be at the point where they are doing it. There are so many important parts that go into getting to your embryo transfer cycle. The agency and your case manager are there to make sure nothing is missed, and your journey goes smoothly, so know that they have the same goal as you do. The team is working to get you there as efficiently as possible. Some things can't be rushed. I would also let intended parents know that there may be bumps in the road to navigate. While science is amazing, it is not perfect. We are dealing with biology, and sometimes, things don't cooperate. From time to time an intended parent might have a failed embryo transfer, or their gestational carrier doesn't respond to medications as they should. When you encounter such hurdles, listen to your fertility doctor, and lean on your case manager to get you over these difficulties. It may take some time, but your team will get you through the trying times as you progress toward creating your family.

From Amanda of Circle Surrogacy:[27]

1. *What do you like about being a case manager for parents going through surrogacy?*

What is there not to like? There is nothing more special than partnering with intended parents on their journey to parenthood. I enjoy teaching them the ins and outs of the process, calming their fears, standing by them during the waiting times that feel like forever, and receiving the photos of them holding their babies for the first time. I especially love when parents

---

27. Circle Surrogacy, www.circlesurrogacy.com, 175 Federal Street, Suite 725, Boston, MA 02110; (617) 439-9900 (Massachusetts office).

come back for a second or third journey, and I can witness the growth of their family over several years. It's a remarkable journey, and I am grateful to play a small part.

2. *What do you think are important qualities and skills for a good case manager?*

A good case manager has the heart for this work, as it is not easy and can be filled with emotional ups and downs. They must be able to listen to the desires and needs of their clients, advocate on their behalf, and proactively problem solve.

3. *What are two or three things you would say to intended parents as advice to go through their surrogacy journey more easily and happily?*

Communication is key. Inviting your case manager in and sharing your plans, hopes, and worries allows them to advocate for you and proactively make decisions to move you closer to your goal. Communication with your surrogate is also vital. Surrogacy is an incredibly emotional and intimate experience. Forming a friendly relationship with your surrogate from the beginning will allow you to share the happy moments and navigate the obstacles successfully. Lastly, I would advise intended parents to recognize that, while they will have the opportunity to make many decisions along the way, there are many aspects of the journey that will be outside their control and outside their case manager's control. Parents often find that the obstacles that once seemed frightening become less so when they can let go.

From Michelle of Simple Surrogacy:

1. *What do you like about being a case manager for parents going through surrogacy?*

As both a five-time surrogate and a medical professional with more than ten years of experience in reproductive endocrinology, I've come to appreciate the overall joy it brings me to help intended parents fulfill their dreams of becoming parents. In some cases, parenthood for our clients can be seen as an intangible dream, so being able to help them fulfill their goals of starting a family is something that I have come to love. As a case manager, you can become very close to the intended parents, creating friendships and close bonds throughout their journey. I've had the pleasure to form close bonds with the most amazing people all over the world, which is something that I wouldn't be able to experience in a different kind of work.

2. *What do you think are important qualities and skills for a good case manager?*

Intended parents rely on case managers greatly during this process to guide them smoothly into each step on their journey. Communication is a large part of being an efficient case manager. Most of our clients are new parents and, therefore, need guidance during all steps of the process, from choosing a surrogate in the very beginning to what items they will need for childcare after their baby is home. Patience and versatility are also quite useful skills for a case manager as not all journeys are free of complications during the process. Being able to provide guidance in a multitude of situations is vital for the clients for a stress-free process.

3. *What are two or three things you would say to intended parents as advice to go through their surrogacy journey more easily and happily?*

While it may be difficult at times, patience is key during this process. Rushing through any part of a surrogate journey doesn't always mean that a baby will come sooner rather than later. We have helped hundreds of clients become parents over the years and, while our efficiency with streamlining the surrogacy process grows, the timeline to complete all the necessary tasks and actions has naturally not greatly changed. Trust is one of the most difficult tasks for intended parents. However, I feel it is very important to have trust during any surrogate journey. I strongly urge our clients to fully trust the medical professionals, their surrogate/donor, our team, and the legal team to guide them in the best way possible. Having reservations with anyone that is a vital part in the process can create difficulties and further tension with an already stressful time in their life. My last piece of advice would be to relinquish control and have an open mind. Control seems to be something that comes naturally with this process given all the decisions that lie in the hands of the intended parents. Clients typically gain a false sense of control given the advances in science and the ability to make specific choices on the overall outcome of their IVF cycle, which is something parents conceiving naturally aren't privy to. From choosing an egg donor with specific qualities to pass on to their children to being able to choose the number of babies likely to be born after an embryo transfer or even the gender of their child(ren) may give a sense of being able to control the outcomes. When parents come in with specific expectations, I try and guide them to have a more open mind and flexible approach when their plans for their future family seem to be unrealistically laid out. We do our best to provide the preferred outcomes for all clients; however, there are many times when the end results are outside our realm of control.

Surrogate Support

Another important aspect of case management is the support given to the surrogates during their surrogacy journeys. The agency should have a system whereby each surrogate is attended to and supported throughout the process of being matched, the pre-pregnancy appointments and process, and the pregnancy and birth. The support does not have to include actual counseling although counseling should become available to the surrogate through a provision in the gestational surrogacy contract with the intended parents.

Mainly, the agency should get to know its surrogates very well and be aware of their personalities and needs in terms of how much communication they would like from their support person. The agency should have, as part of their routine operations, a system to make sure that every surrogate receives communication from the agency support team on a regular, consistent basis.

The support team should know the dates of all the medical appointments the surrogate must attend and all the travel that is planned for the surrogate to go to the IVF clinic for medical evaluation and for the embryo transfer. In addition, the agency support team should know where the surrogate is being medically monitored during her pre-embryo transfer cycle and should keep in close contact with the surrogate about how the monitoring is going.

Although surrogates are independent and capable, they also are allowing themselves to be very vulnerable by exposing their medical histories, family and personal backgrounds, home life, marriage, and much more to the scrutiny of the agency screening process, the intended parents, and the IVF physician, nurses, and administrators. The surrogate support team must keep this in mind and realize that the surrogate may need and, in fact, deserves the utmost attention and care as she prepares to give of herself both physically and emotionally to bring a baby into the world for the intended parents. It is the work of the agency to make the most diligent efforts in understanding what the surrogacy process means to each surrogate.

One potentially very positive aspect of a surrogacy agency is that, almost always, it has experienced gestational surrogates as part of its team. These women know firsthand what it means to be a surrogate. They understand the commitment as well as the physical and emotional contributions that it takes to be a surrogate. They also understand how the surrogate's family is involved and that all members of the surrogate's family are impacted. These experienced agency team members can assist the surrogates in explaining things to their children, friends, and relatives. They are also empathic and caring toward intended parents because they have given birth to their intended parents' babies, and they have seen first-hand the joys and struggles of intended parents. Experienced surrogates can be instrumental in forming an effective, responsive, and caring surrogate support team.

Legal Supervision

Gestational surrogacy is legally complex. Chapter 12, "The Gestational Surrogacy Agreement," will focus on the laws and legal procedures of surrogacy, but there should also be a focus on the surrogacy agency's role in managing the legal matters involved in the journey.

Focusing on the law is crucial in the matching process because not all intended parents may be matched in every surrogacy-friendly state. The agency team must be aware of the laws that will be applied to each surrogacy journey and review the laws with a competent lawyer to make sure the intended parents will be able to establish their legal parentage in the jurisdiction (state) where their baby will be born. The case manager is not expected to know the law of every state in the United States, but she must have resources to help with finding the answers to make a legally appropriate match. The most effective and experienced surrogacy agencies will have either a lawyer on staff or a very close working relationship with a competent surrogacy lawyer to attend to these legal matters.

Intended parents need lawyers throughout the process. The first contract they may sign is the retainer contract with the surrogacy agency. If they desire to have this contract reviewed by a lawyer who is independent from the surrogacy agency, they should go ahead and do this. Not every intended parent has the surrogacy agency retainer contract reviewed by independent counsel, but it is important that they know they have this opportunity and right to do this if they want to have the retainer agreement reviewed by an independent lawyer of their choice.

The next important legal matters are the gestational surrogacy agreement with the surrogate and, if an egg donor and/or sperm donor are involved, there must be egg donation and sperm donation agreements. As to the gestational surrogacy agreement, the intended parents will often utilize the services of the agency lawyer or a lawyer that they choose outside of the agency. The most important aspect of choice of lawyer is that she or he is experienced in assisted reproduction technology law. The surrogate will also have a lawyer who will be independent and outside the agency or the law firm being used by the intended parents. This lawyer will review the gestational surrogacy agreement and provide advice, guidance, and legal representation for the surrogate.

There is a question of conflict of interest if the intended parents are using a lawyer who is on the staff of the agency. This is because the lawyer works for the agency that is also recruiting and getting to know the gestational surrogates who are being matched with intended parents through the agency. If this potential conflict of interest is disclosed and the intended parents freely understand and accept the lawyer's involvement with the agency, the intended parents may choose to accept the representation by the agency lawyer. However, they should know that they have choices, and they may select a different lawyer to represent them in the drafting and negotiating of the surrogacy agreement.

Also, the prebirth order of legal parentage, or in some cases the post-birth order, is another legal matter that must be addressed. A lawyer in the state where the birth will occur will be responsible for this legal proceeding. Once again, the agency team often coordinates this and makes referrals to the lawyer who will do the legal work to establish the parental rights of the intended parents.

The agency team will be fully informed about these legal matters and should stay in communication with the lawyers doing the legal work on the agreements and prebirth or post-birth orders establishing parental rights, especially to make sure the legal work is getting done in a timely manner. It is most important that the prebirth order is obtained prior to the birth of the baby. These legal orders or decrees must then be provided to the hospital where the birth will take place, and the state department of vital records that will issue the birth certificate with the designation of the intended parents as the legal parents of the baby.

The agency should be making sure this happens on time prior to the birth of the baby. In the rare cases of post-birth orders, the agency should be making sure that the legal work is commenced prior to the birth and concluded as soon as possible after the birth.

Escrow Management

An escrow agent is a person or entity that holds property in trust for third parties while a transaction is finalized or a disagreement is resolved. The escrow agent has a fiduciary responsibility to both parties of the escrow agreement. James Chen's Investopedia article defines *escrow agent* as follows:

Key takeaways:
- An escrow agent is a third party, a person or entity, which holds an asset or funds before they are transferred from one party wto another.
- The escrow agent holds the funds or the asset until both parties have fulfilled their contractual requirements.
- Escrow agents are often associated with real estate transactions, but they can be used in any situation where funds will pass from one party to another.[28]

Julia Kagan's *Investopedia* article defines *fiduciary* as follows:

> A fiduciary is a person or organization that acts on behalf of another person or persons, putting their clients' interest ahead of their own, with a duty to preserve good faith and trust. Being a fiduciary thus requires being bound both legally and ethically to act in the other's best interests.[29]

Adam Barone's *Investopedia* article defines *fiduciary duty* as follows:

> A fiduciary duty exists in law when a person or entity places trust, confidence, and reliance on another to exercise discretion or expertise in acting on behalf of the client. The fiduciary must knowingly accept that trust and confidence. In the US legal system, a fiduciary duty describes a relationship between two parties that obligates one to act solely in the interest of the other. The party designated as the fiduciary owes a legal duty to a principal,

---

28. James Chen, "Escrow Agent: Explanation in Real Estate," *Investopedia*, December 30, 2020, https://www.investopedia.com/terms/e/escrow_agent.asp.

29. Julia Kagan, "Fiduciary Definition: Examples and Why They Are Important," *Investopedia*, September 15, 2022, https://www.investopedia.com/terms/f/fiduciary.asp.

and strict care must be taken to ensure that no conflict of interest arises between the fiduciary and the principal.[30]

In surrogacy matters, the principals are the intended parents, and the escrow agent is the fiduciary who owes a fiduciary duty to the intended parents. The work and the responsibility of the escrow agent are very critical and serious. The intended parents must be satisfied that their escrow agent is competent, knowledgeable, ethical, insured, and trustworthy to hold large sums of money and manage these funds in a manner that is in the best interests of the intended parents. Also, in surrogacy matters, it is important to seek and find an escrow agent who is knowledgeable about surrogacy because one of the functions of the escrow agent in a surrogacy arrangement is to be aware of and fully familiar with the gestational surrogacy agreement, as that will be the document that will dictate the disbursement of funds.

In surrogacy arrangements, the intended parents must deposit enough money to be able to pay the gestational surrogate her compensation throughout the pregnancy and for other expenses as well. The key is that a third party will handle the funds and be responsible for the payments to be made to the surrogate with the approval of the intended parents and according to the contract between the intended parents and the surrogate.

As part of its case management functions, the agency team will be fully aware of the escrow account, the account balance, and the payment obligations under the gestational surrogacy agreement. In some cases, the escrow management account will be under the umbrella of the surrogacy agency organization, while in other cases, the escrow management will be done by a third-party escrow program outside the surrogacy agency.

The Society for Ethics in Egg Donation and Surrogacy (SEEDS)[31] is an organization that includes members that are egg donation and surrogacy agencies. SEEDS sets forth standards for its member organizations, and one of the standards covers escrow management. It provides as follows:

All unearned or undisbursed funds belonging to intended parents, surrogates, or donors must be held in either:

a. an escrow account held by a licensed escrow company with a minimum bond (crime policy) greater than the amount of funds held in all escrow accounts and not controlled by the agency associated with the journey; or

b. a law firm's client trust or escrow account maintained by an attorney with the proper disclosures and conflict waivers where applicable (e.g., when the

---

30. Adam Barone, "What Is a Fiduciary Duty? Examples and Types Evaluated," *Investopedia*, May 24, 2023, https://www.investopedia.com/ask/answers/042915/what-are-some-examples-fiduciary-duty.asp.

31. Society for Ethics in Egg Donation and Surrogacy, https://www.seedsethics.org.

attorney holding escrow also represents one or all participants in any of the legal services).[32]

The reasoning behind this standard is that the funds belonging to the intended parents must be protected. Nonlawyers who hold escrow accounts must be licensed and bonded to protect funds against fraud, theft, cyberattacks, and other such vulnerabilities. The exception for lawyers is because lawyers' trust accounts are subject to scrutiny by overseeing authorities such as state bar regulations as well as laws and codes of ethics that apply to lawyers.

What is meant by conflict of interest? As explained earlier, the surrogacy agency team will get to know the surrogate applicants as they go through the application and screening processes. The recruiting team at the agency get to know the surrogates well, and the team will develop relationships with these women. That is normal and good, as it is important for the agency to know its surrogates as well as possible and be confident that the surrogates are good, sound, stable people committed to gestational surrogacy.

However, in contrast to this, escrow agents must separate themselves from surrogates and abide solely by the terms of the contract. For example, if a surrogate thinks she is entitled to lost wages, but the intended parents are not sure, the escrow agent must not side with the surrogate. The escrow agent must act in the best interests of the intended parents, as it is their money the escrow agent is holding. In a case such as this, the surrogate should be advised to discuss the matter with the lawyer who assisted her with her gestational surrogacy contract, and the lawyer for the intended parents must discuss the question of the payment with the surrogate's lawyer. Such an example demonstrates why escrow management is serious and must be addressed by knowledgeable, trustworthy, experienced professionals. The point is that the intended parents must feel and believe their money is safe and protected and will only be used for legitimate needs and expenses during the surrogacy journey. In the case of a dispute, all parties must be encouraged to work toward a resolution.

All of these pieces—the case management team, the surrogate support, the legal supervision, and the escrow management—are interconnected and will be involved under the case management functions of the surrogacy agency team.

---

32. Society for Ethics in Egg Donation and Surrogacy, https://www.seedsethics.org/Published Standards.

8

What Is Independent Matching?

Independent matching is a term applied to the matching of intended parents and surrogates without the assistance, coordination, and oversight of a surrogacy agency. When people are faced with infertility, or if they are a gay couple or single intended parent, they may desire or need to keep costs as low as possible, and therefore, they will be looking for ways to reduce costs. One way to do this is to have a surrogate who is a good friend or relative and who will not be seeking compensation for the surrogacy. Another cost-reducing possibility is to avoid the surrogacy agency fee by independently searching for and matching with a surrogate. Intended parents do this by placing their own ads or by participating on social media sites available for this purpose.

Using a Friend or Relative as a Gestational Surrogate

One form of independent matching with a surrogate is when the intended parents have a friend or relative who will be their surrogate. This sometimes happens when people around the intended parents are aware that there is an infertility concern, or they are aware that a gay couple or gay individual would like to start a family using a surrogate. This is when a friend or relative may step up and offer to become the gestational surrogate for the intended parents.

This is a very big decision for a potential surrogate to make, and when the offer first occurs, it is important that the intended parents do not get overly excited about it. This is because often, when the person who steps up starts to consider the seriousness of going through gestational surrogacy and begins to really think about visits to a reproductive clinic, taking injectable medications, and taking on the physical and emotional aspects of a pregnancy as a surrogate, she may back out. This can lead to disappointment, frustration, and even frayed relationships between the intended parents and the woman who was considering being their surrogate.

Sometimes, these arrangements will work out beautifully. A woman might be a gestational surrogate for her sister. Or she may have a gay brother and become the gestational surrogate for her gay brother and his partner who are creating embryos using the sperm from her brother's partner. There are times when a good friend will become a surrogate for intended parents, and these matches also often work out well.

In such situations that seem promising, there are some initial steps that should be taken. First, the parties to an independent match must participate in the counseling or psychological evaluations that are routinely done in surrogacy screening and matching to maximize the potential for a positive and fulfilling journey and to minimize the risk of disagreements during pre-pregnancy, pregnancy, or post-pregnancy. They should engage in counseling with a mental health provider who specializes in assisted reproduction, infertility, and surrogacy. They may feel certain they want to proceed and suggest there is no need for this, but a trained counselor can greatly help to lay a stable foundation for the surrogacy journey and to make the process more fulfilling, rewarding, and emotionally successful for everyone.

Next, the surrogate must go to the fertility clinic and be medically screened. The reproductive physician will review the surrogate's medical records from her pregnancies and her obstetrical history and will physically examine the surrogate to see if she is medically able to proceed to the embryo transfer and pregnancy.

Some medical clinics may require that intended parents who enter into an independent match with a surrogate also engage a surrogacy agency in order to have the support, supervision, and coordination that a reputable and experienced surrogacy agency will provide. In this case, the intended parents should interview surrogacy agencies to see if they will offer a program of support although the agency is not doing the actual matching with the surrogate. If so, some questions will have to be answered. Will the agency reduce its agency fee since it does not have to match the intended parents with the surrogate? Also, what will the scope of services look like? Agencies are used to doing comprehensive screening of surrogate applicants. Has some of the screening been done by the reproductive clinic? How much screening is left to do? The answers to these important questions enable the intended parents and the surrogacy agency to make sure that they each have a good, *written* understanding of what is expected of the agency as well as the detailed obligations of the intended parents.

Can I Search for a Surrogate without Agency Help?

Is it possible for intended parents to find their own surrogate without the assistance of a surrogacy matching agency? The answer is yes. In the event the intended parents do not have a friend or relative stepping up to be their surrogate, they may still try to independently match. However, they will have the same risks as outlined above when intended parents independently match with a known surrogate. Also, there will be increased risks because now the intended parents are meeting an unknown person and engaging with a new person about whom the intended parents know little or nothing. Keep in mind that people are coming together for an incredibly important and profound endeavor—that is, to work as a group to achieve a pregnancy and bring a baby into the world.

Having a baby through surrogacy is very complicated and requires experienced professionals to assist with the myriad of legal and medical details. The vulnerabilities of all parties are immense. The intended parents place their hopes and dreams, their faith and trust, in a woman they most likely meet on the Internet. The gestational surrogate must place her trust, her emotional and physical well-being, and her expectation of fair compensation in the hands of intended parents about whom she knows little or nothing.

While this can work and has worked for people who meet in this way and who create independent matches, it is very important that people consider and face the risks and manage the risks in order to minimize them. No one should enter such an independent match without the expectation and organization of psychological and medical screening, getting to know each other well, participating in counseling sessions together, and exchanging verified information of a personal nature.

By way of analogy, let me describe the one time I tried to sell my home without a real estate agent. I am a lawyer, and I believed I could successfully market and sell my own property without the help of a real estate agent. By doing this I would save the commission I would otherwise pay the agent. On the day of my open house, the first prospective buyers came into the house, went down to the basement, came back out, and told me I had about four inches of water in the basement. The hot water heater had failed and flooded the basement. I was beyond stressed. I called a cleanup crew, got the repairs done, and proceeded to list the house with a real estate agent. The agent did all the work to get the house sold and I simply had to answer questions and sign documents. It was a huge relief!

Selling real estate is not nearly as profound or emotional as having a baby through surrogacy, including making embryos, achieving a pregnancy, and experiencing the birth of the baby. For many, it may be better to work with a surrogacy agency and enjoy the benefits and assistance that such a team will bring to the surrogacy experience.

Another question is: Who are the women who are advertising to become surrogates through independent matching? Again, there are some concerns that need to be considered. Why would these women not want the support and presence of a surrogacy agency? Are they women who have not been qualified under agency screening and, therefore, must try to match with intended parents independently? There are many scams on the Internet. People must be careful. Intended parents must be careful about putting too much hope up front in a potential surrogate they connect with online. And surrogates must be careful, as intended parents also are not being supported or evaluated by a surrogacy agency. Again, this is not to say these arrangements cannot work. Many can and do work, but the emphasis is about getting the comprehensive screening done whether there is an agency involved or not.

9

Anticipated Fees and Costs of Gestational Surrogacy

The surrogacy agency, the IVF fertility clinic, the egg donation agency and/ or the sperm or egg bank will have documentation showing the anticipated expenses for the services and procedures that are required or requested by the intended parents. The endeavor to have a child through gestational surrogacy is complex and costly. The intended parents need and deserve details of the itemized costs that they will incur throughout the journey. Here is an outline together with estimates of these expenses with the caveat that what is written here is current as of the writing of this edition. Because of advances in medical technology and the favorable evolution of laws, gestational surrogacy in the United States, although expensive, continues to become increasingly popular. Therefore, the demand for surrogates is increasing and, as a result, fees, and costs are on the rise.

Surrogate Compensation

The intended parents and the gestational carrier and her spouse, if she is married, will enter into a highly detailed gestational surrogacy agreement. This agreement, also known as the gestational surrogacy contract, will provide a specific list of itemized expenses that will go toward the compensation for the surrogate.

There are many components to this agreement, and one major one is the surrogate's base compensation. This is the amount that will be paid to the surrogate, usually in equal monthly installments, during the pregnancy. These payments will begin with the confirmation of pregnancy.

Today, an estimated base compensation for a first-time gestational surrogate will be around $45,000 to $50,000. There are variations on this. For example, if a surrogate has medical insurance that will cover the surrogate pregnancy, she may request an additional $5,000 in her base compensation. If she is an experienced surrogate, her base compensation will most likely be increased to $55,000 or $60,000. If she is carrying twins, there will be an addition to the base compensation of at least $5,000 to $10,000. It is also important to note that the surrogates state what their desired compensation is and, therefore, what is stated here may change from case to case.

There are standards in surrogacy agreements, and according to these standards, there will usually be the following additional payments (that are negotiable) to or on behalf of the surrogate:

Travel Expenses (if applicable)

- economy airfare for the surrogate and a companion
- economy rental car
- hotel accommodations
- transportation (taxi, ride hailing, rental car service, etc.)
- meals and necessary incidentals when traveling
- mileage

Maternity Clothes

- $750 for singleton pregnancy; additional $250 for twin pregnancy

Monthly Allowance

- $300 to $350 per month, starting the month following contract signing with the intended parents through the duration of gestational surrogacy agreement. This is intended to cover expenses incurred by the surrogate such as mileage, tolls, parking, and local transportation for routine medical appointments; childcare and lost wages for routine medical appointments (usually excluding screening/testing and embryo transfer travel to the IVF clinic); nonprescription medications, vitamins, and supplements; postage and fax charges; long-distance phone charges; insurance copays; and any miscellaneous or out-of-pocket expenses not specifically listed in the surrogacy contract.

Housekeeping

- Housekeeping during periods of physician-ordered bed rest or physician-ordered restricted activity and for post-birth recuperation weeks
- Childcare during periods of physician-ordered bed rest or physician-ordered restricted activity, surrogacy-related travel (e.g., testing/transfer travel), and the surrogate's hospitalization for the birth

Lost Wages

- Lost earnings during periods of physician-ordered bed rest or physician-ordered restricted activity, pre-cycle testing, embryo transfer if traveling out of town, and the post-birth recovery period
- Spouse's net lost wages (if applicable)

Regarding lost wages, many agreements have a limit or cap on this amount. The limits range from approximately $5,000 to $20,000. If there is no cap on lost wages, then the agreement must be very specific, detailed, and clear regarding what circumstances will trigger payment of lost wages. In a healthy pregnancy, a higher cap may not be reached because the surrogate will be paid lost wages for two trips to the clinic (the testing/screening appointment and the embryo transfer trip) and for several weeks to recuperate after the delivery and birth. Additional lost wages will be due if there are pregnancy complications and the treating physician orders bedrest or restricted activity for the surrogate. One of the reasons a multiple pregnancy may include increased costs is because the surrogate may be more likely to require bedrest and, therefore, additional lost wages.

Examples of other contingent expenses that are often listed in gestational surrogacy agreements include the following (these are estimates and may vary in different proposed agreements):

- $3,000 for a C-section
- $2,000 for termination of the pregnancy due to a fetal abnormality
- $2,000 for selective reduction of a multiple pregnancy
- $500 for certain invasive medical procedures (per procedure)
- $250 for a mock cycle (a rarely performed practice cycle to see how the surrogate's uterine lining develops)
- $1,000 for amniocentesis (invasive test to check for fetal abnormalities)
- $4,000 for partial loss of reproductive organs (a rare occurrence)
- $8,000 for full loss of reproductive organs (a rare occurrence)
- $150/week for breastmilk (if agreed to by the parties) and the actual cost for breastmilk supplies and shipping costs
- up to approximately $1,000 for psychological counseling and support (during pregnancy/post-birth, to be paid only upon submission of receipts or invoices)

This list of extra payments, as well as the specified amounts to the surrogate shown here, will vary on a case-by-case basis. Some contracts may have additional items of compensation, and some may have fewer or different items of compensation. It is simply important to realize that, incorporated in the surrogacy agreement, there will be these kinds of potential extra payment to be made to the surrogate.

There will also be a payment of $750 to $1,000 for each embryo transfer. This may be broken up into installments: $250 when the surrogate begins injectable medication; and the remainder when the embryo transfer is performed. There may also be bonus payments depending on the program and the compensation package. For example, there may be a signing bonus of approximately $500. Again, what is important is that the intended parents and the surrogate are aware of the compensation terms that will be included in the gestational surrogacy agreement.

Agency Fees

The surrogacy agency will charge a fee for its services, and this fee will most likely include recruiting qualified, available surrogates to be matched with the intended parents; providing consulting, advice, and assistance to the parents in choosing their surrogate; coordinating and supporting the surrogacy journey for the parents and the surrogate; and other services. Most likely this will be a flat fee ranging from approximately $25,000 to $35,000, with some variations on amount and payment terms and other expenses.

Some agencies will offer an all-inclusive package that will include agency fee, screening fees, surrogate compensation and other fees and expenses. It will be important, when evaluating these programs, that there is transparency as to what is covered in the payments to the agency. Some agencies will require a deposit when the intended parents sign on. The remainder of the agency fee will become due later, for example, after the match with a surrogate is confirmed. Other payment models may include paying a greater amount up front, some of which may go into the parents' escrow account, or no payment at all until there is a match with a surrogate.

What is important is that the intended parents are made aware of the agency fees and the payment schedule in writing as well as potential additional fees and expenses. For example, a small percentage of intended parents may need a second surrogate because their first surrogate did not get pregnant, or she encountered a medical problem or other unforeseen circumstance rendering her unable to continue as a surrogate. The intended parents need to know in advance whether there will be a rematch fee to the agency for matching the parents with this second surrogate.

Most importantly, the intended parents must ask and ascertain what the agency fee covers. What is the scope of the work that the agency proposes it will do for the fee it is charging? This should be clearly outlined and defined in the agency's retainer agreement. With that in mind, intended parents should not be looking at the cost in terms of which agency is the least expensive. Rather, they should evaluate the fee as it relates to the work that the agency says it will be doing. A comprehensive surrogacy agency should state in its retainer that it will be on board from the date of the retainer through the birth of the intended parents' baby, providing information, guidance, support, and assistance throughout the journey. An agency that is not comprehensive may match the intended parents with a surrogate but be less available or not available at all for continuing surrogacy journey.

Another factor is the size and experience of the agency team. Does the agency provide a team of experienced, knowledgeable case managers and a surrogate support team? Does the agency fee include an available attorney to answer legal questions and supervise the legal matters that will be a necessary aspect of the surrogacy journey? The point is that it is not just about the amount of the fee but, more importantly, what the intended parents are getting for the fees paid.

In addition, the intended parents must be apprised as to whether there is a refund policy. There may be a short-term initial period when a refund may be given to the intended parents, but once the agency begins its intensive work on behalf of the intended parents, the payments will nonrefundable.

Legal Fees

There are some major areas of legal work that go into the surrogacy journey. The first is the gestational surrogacy contract. This is drafted by the intended parents' lawyer. The fee for the drafting of this agreement may range from $2,500 to $3,500. Once the initial draft is done and approved by the intended parents, the contract will be forwarded to the attorney representing the surrogate. This attorney's fee will be approximately $1,500 to $2,500.

During the pregnancy, the lawyer located in the state where the birth is to take place will do the prebirth or post-birth order of legal parentage. The legal fees for this work range approximately from $2,500 to $4,000.

Other potential legal fees may be incurred for the drafting and review of an egg donation agreement, a sperm donation agreement, or an embryo disposition agreement as well as for a home-country lawyer for international parents who may need legal advice as to immigration or travel visa matters, establishing citizenship for their baby in their home country, and parental rights for the intended parents in their home country.

Another area where intended parents most likely will incur legal fees is in estate planning. When there is a pregnancy, the intended parents should complete their wills, powers of attorney, and appointments of guardians and trustees for their children. These fees may be $500 to $1,500 for simple and standard documents, but such fees may escalate depending on the nature and size of the intended parents' estates and if they need estate and tax planning advice.

IVF Clinic

Intended parents must engage an IVF clinic where they will create their embryos with the assistance and supervision of their chosen reproductive physician (fertility specialist). At first, they will plan how they will create their embryos. If the intended parents are a straight couple, they must decide if they will use their own eggs and sperm to create their embryos or if they will need donor gametes. If the intended parents are a gay male couple, they most likely will create embryos using sperm from both, together with donor eggs. Single intended parents also turn to surrogacy to have children. If the intended parent is a man, he will need an egg donor to create his embryos. If the intended parent is a woman, she will need a sperm donor to create embryos.

At the IVF clinic, the following procedures will be planned and eventually carried out depending on the needs of the intended parents:

1. Semen analysis;
2. Medical screening of egg donor;

3. Medical screening of surrogate;

4. Egg retrieval (medical procedure to extract the developed eggs from the ovaries of the egg donor);

5. In vitro fertilization (laboratory procedure where sperm and eggs are combined to create embryos);

6. Freezing of the embryos for preservation until they are used for the embryo transfer procedure;

7. Surrogate's first visit to the IVF clinic for physical examination and commencement of medication to stimulate the development of her uterine lining;

8. Surrogate's second visit to the IVF clinic for the embryo transfer;

9. Embryo transfer (medical procedure to insert embryos into the uterus of the surrogate); and

10. Medical monitoring of the first twelve weeks of the surrogate pregnancy.

Egg Donation

If the intended parents need an egg donor, fees and expenses for and related to egg donation will vary. Some intended parents may have a known egg donor for whom no compensation is required. For example, an intended mother may have the benefit of using her sister's eggs. If her sister is biologically/genetically related to her, this is a welcome scenario because now she will be using eggs with which she has a genetic connection. Other intended parents may have the benefit of having eggs donated by a friend or relative who is not seeking compensation. However, there will be donor screening costs for medical, psychological, and genetic testing. There may be travel expenses for flights and hotel when the egg donor goes to the IVF medical clinic for screening and for the egg retrieval. If the egg donor is chosen from an egg donation agency instead of through the medical clinic, there will also me an egg donation agency fee.

For any arrangement with an egg donor, whether she is known or unknown, and whether she will be compensated, there will be legal fees. There must be an egg donation agreement drafted by a lawyer who is knowledgeable about egg donation, and there will be a legal fee for this, and there will be a need for a lawyer to review the agreement on behalf of the egg donor and to represent and advise her. There will also be an expense for egg donation complications insurance to cover the medical expenses in case the donor has medical complications related to the egg donation procedures.

Sperm Donation

Using a sperm donor will cost less than using an egg donor. The sperm donor undergoes much less medically intrusive procedures. If he is donating through a cryobank or a medical clinic, he will be screened for a comprehensive health history. In addition, he will undergo the following screening:

1. Psychological evaluation;
2. Semen analysis;
3. Physical examination;
4. Infectious disease testing;
5. Interviews in person with staff;
6. Educational degree verification by reviewing certified transcripts; and
7. Criminal background investigation.

The cost of donated sperm varies based on personal needs, but must at least include the costs of vials of sperm and shipping. The items that must be considered in terms of the fees for using a sperm donor include vials of semen specimens, access to profiles—that is, whether the recipient would prefer to see a basic or full access profile, shipping costs of the containers to the recipients' medical clinic, donor selection and/or genetic consultations, lab services, and storage.

Recipients may want to purchase several vials to have enough for several cycles and for more than one baby. In case the recipient parents want to have more than one child and they want their children to be genetically related, they will want to store some vials with their reproductive clinic. If they do not do this, they run the risk that the sperm donor they have selected will not be available when they want to have their second child.

In the event the recipient parents use a donor who is not chosen from a cryobank, they will need to have a sperm donation agreement, and they must discuss screening of the donor and the costs of screening with their reproductive physician. Legal contracts for sperm donation are not complicated, and they should not be expensive to prepare, but they are important and necessary.

Additional Legal Fees for International Intended Parents

Intended parents who live outside the United States and come to the United States to have their children through gestational surrogacy must have an experienced family formation lawyer or immigration lawyer in their home country to provide legal advice regarding the citizenship of their children in the home country. Each foreign country has its own rules and requirements that intended parents must know and follow to return home with legal safety and certainty to establish their legal parentage and the baby's citizenship in the home country. Legal procedures in each country vary, levels of service vary, and therefore, legal fees vary.

Insurance Costs and Expenses

As many US citizens know, health insurance matters are complex in the United States. There are many different insurance companies, and each company has many different health insurance plans. Each insurance plan will have multiple components of fees and expenses that are not covered by the actual insurance. These include the premium,[33] which is the cost of insurance.

Another component of insurance costs is the deductible:

A health insurance deductible is the amount of money you pay out of pocket for healthcare services covered under your insurance plan before your plan begins to pay benefits for eligible expenses. The amount you pay for a health insurance deductible is determined by the type of health insurance plan you have and your coverage benefits. As a rule, the higher your premium, the lower your deductible is likely to be. Similarly, a higher deductible can result in a lower monthly premium. Your monthly premium is the fee you pay on a recurring basis to your health insurance company to provide you with coverage.[34]

Two more components of expenses related to medical insurance include copays and unreimbursed medical expenses. "A co-pay is a fixed out-of-pocket amount paid by an insured for covered services. It is a standard part of many health insurance plans. Insurance providers often charge co-pays for services such as doctor visits or prescription drugs. Co-pays are a specified dollar amount rather than a percentage of the bill, and they are usually paid at the time of service."[35] Copay amounts vary but they are usually around $25 or less.

Unreimbursed medical expenses are the portions of medical bills that are not covered or paid by insurance. These are also out-of-pocket expenses to the intended parents, and they are payable after the medical treatment is provided and a bill or invoice is sent out by the provider to the patient and to the insurance company. If the insurance policy will cover the expense, but not the entire bill, there will be a portion called the unreimbursed medical bill that must be paid by the intended parents

The term *unreimbursed medical expenses* may also be used as a catch-all phrase for expenses that include medical bills not paid for by insurance, copays, and deductibles. In this context, however, it is best to separate out the various components of insurance expenses to provide some clarity as to where the various items of expense come from in the overall medical billing system.

---

33. "An insurance premium is the amount of money an individual or business pays for an insurance policy. Insurance premiums are paid for policies that cover health care, auto, home, and life insurance. Once earned, the premium is income for the insurance company. It also represents a liability, as the insurer must provide coverage for claims being made against the policy. Failure to pay the premium on the part of the individual or the business may result in the cancellation of the policy." See Julia Kagan, "Insurance Premium Defined, How It's Calculated, and Types, *Investopedia*, updated March 3, 2022, https://www.investopedia.com/terms/i/insurance-premium.asp.

34. Rebecca Lake, "Health Insurance Deductible: What It Is and How It Works," *Investopedia*, January 2, 2023, https://www.investopedia.com/health-insurance-deductible-4773113.

35. Julia Kagan, "What Is a Copay? Definition in Health Insurance and Example," *Investopedia*, July 18, 2021, https://www.investopedia.com/terms/c/copay.asp.

There are various insurances that must be discussed and that must be in place for the surrogacy arrangement. They are health insurance for the surrogate to cover the surrogate pregnancy, delivery, and birth; egg donor complications insurance if there is an egg donor; term life insurance for the surrogate; and newborn insurance.

Many surrogates have medical insurance for themselves and their families, but these policies must be reviewed to see if they will cover a surrogate pregnancy. Unfortunately, there are many insurance policies that, although they cover pregnancy, do not cover pregnancy if the insured is pregnant as a surrogate. A good resource for the review of insurance policies is ART Risk Financial and Insurance Solutions,[36] a reputable and experienced insurance resource for assisted reproduction matters and surrogacy. If the surrogate does not have a health insurance plan to cover a surrogate pregnancy, a plan will have to be purchased, and the intended parents will pay the premiums for this health insurance.

Often, the health insurance, if needed, is obtained through the Patient Protection and Affordable Care Act (a/k/a "ACA" or "Obamacare"). These policies may be purchased during the special enrollment periods and usually cost approximately $500 to $700 per month. Intended parents should be prepared to pay these premiums for some period over a year and a half. Note that the current New York Child Parent Security Act requires intended parents to pay for their surrogate's insurance from the time of the confirmed match with the surrogate until twelve months following the birth of the baby.

Health insurance costs may cost more than $30,000 or more for a Lloyd's of London surrogacy insurance policy. There is also a backup plan or contingency plan for health insurance, also through Lloyd's of London. This is often purchased when the surrogate has her own insurance, but there is some risk with respect to the certainty of whether the health insurance policy that she has will cover the surrogate pregnancy. A deposit of approximately $2,500 to $3,000 is required to have the backup insurance available. If a need for insurance arises in that the surrogate's insurance carrier denies coverage, the backup plan may be accessed but, when it is activated, it will require an additional premium (payment) and it will have a high retention amount or deductible.

All intended parents must have or obtain health insurance for their newborn baby that will be effective from the moment the baby is born. Intended parents who reside in the United States may already have medical insurance for their own health care, and they can simply add their baby to the health insurance policy at the time of birth. If the baby is born outside the state of the parents' residence, the insurance must be reviewed to make sure it will cover a baby born outside of the state where her/his parents live. Parents who do not have medical insurance that they can use for their newborn baby must obtain such insurance. Domestic intended parents may get a health insurance

---

36. ART Risk, https://artrisksolutions.com.

policy for their newborn upon the birth of the baby. This is possible because the intended parents are citizens and residents of the United States.

International intended parents who live abroad will not be able to obtain newborn insurance through the Affordable Health Care Act at the time of the birth of their baby unless they are residents of the United States and they obtain newborn health insurance. This is most important for international intended parents because they often do not have global insurance or private insurance.

Costs for such policies for newborns vary widely. For international parents who desire to try to have twins and who do not have private or global medical insurance for their babies born in the United States, the cost for insurance for twins may be as high as $90,000[37]. There are resources for international intended parents to find information about the cost of newborn insurance. A surrogacy agency should be able to assist international intended parents in figuring out how they will obtain health insurance for their newborn.

---

37. ART Risk, "Newborn Insurance Options," https://artrisksolutions.com/newborn-insurance-options/

PART II

The Journey

10

Stages of the Surrogacy Journey

Stage 1: Matching

There are three major stages of the surrogacy journey. The first stage is matching. This is when the surrogacy agency should be communicating regularly with the intended parents to apprise them and give them updates as to how the recruiting and search is going for their surrogate. At a certain point during this stage, the agency's matching coordinator will begin to present profiles of surrogate candidates to the waiting intended parents. Parents should be able to decline a candidate for any reason, but if they are interested in a profile, then the agency will inform them of the myriad of details about the surrogate.

To clarify, matching with a surrogate is not like matching with an egg donor or sperm donor. Surrogates do not wait on databases to be chosen. Since there is a demand for them, they are pre-matched with intended parents while going through screening. When the screening is completed successfully, and if the intended parents maintain their interest in this surrogate candidate, a meeting will be arranged for the surrogate and the intended parents. Usually, as a surrogate is progressing through the screening process, the agency team is getting to know her very well because they are assisting her with making the screening appointments, giving her instructions on next steps in the process, answering her questions about surrogacy, and providing her with support.

As the recruiting team is getting to know her, they are also assessing whether she is likely to successfully complete the screening. The agency team is also working on getting to know the intended parents who are waiting to be matched, and further, which surrogates in the screening process may be good matches for those intended parents. This is the time when they will begin proposing candidates to their intended parents. The demand for surrogates and the rigorous screening are the reasons for the waiting period when it comes to matching.

Matching Criteria

There are many different factors, both objective and subjective, that go into matching intended parents with surrogates. It is the work of the agency to get to know the intended parents and surrogates so that the wish lists of the parents and the surrogate candidates can be reasonably satisfied. The matching process begins with a careful review of the profiles submitted by the intended parents and surrogates where they outline what they are looking for, and hoping for in the match.

For parents, the matching considerations will include, although not be limited to, the following:

1. Do they want to transfer one embryo or two? In other words, do they want to try to conceive a twin pregnancy?

2. Do they want to terminate the pregnancy if there is a fetal abnormality?

3. Where does the surrogate live and what are the legal procedures in her state of residence?

4. Is the surrogate married or single and do the intended parents have a preference in this regard?

5. How many children does she have and what are their ages? For some parents, they may want the surrogate to have older children, so she is not busy lifting small children. For others, this may not matter.

6. What is the age of the surrogate?

7. What are her attitudes and behaviors regarding nutrition and healthy eating?

8. Does she work and, if so, what kind of work does she do?

9. Does she have medical insurance that will cover a surrogate pregnancy? If she does not, how will insurance be put in place and how much will it cost?

10. How much communication do the intended parents and surrogates hope for or expect during the journey? It is normal and natural to want a good deal of consistent communication, especially during the pregnancy. Will the surrogate be willing to be in close communication about the pregnancy?

11. Do the intended parents and surrogate have thoughts on what kind of a relationship they may want or not want after the birth? This is difficult to address during the matching period because people do not yet know each other. But sometimes parents may know ahead of time that they do not want or cannot continue a relationship with the surrogate after the birth. This is generally the case with some international intended parents because surrogacy is illegal or taboo in their home countries, so they express a preference not to carry on a relationship after the birth.

Surrogates may consider the following:

1. Will the intended parents desire to transfer one embryo or two? The surrogate will usually have a preference as to whether she wants only one embryo to be transferred or if she is open to trying to carry twins.

2. Will she go along with the wishes of the intended parents if they want to terminate a pregnancy for a fetal abnormality?

3. Where do the intended parents live? Will she consider carrying for an international intended parent or couple?

4. Will she carry for a single intended parent? Will she carry for a couple?

5. Will she carry for a gay or straight couple?

6. Will she carry for an HIV-positive intended parent?

7. What are the intended parents like? What kinds of work do they do?

8. What do they do for fun and recreation?

9. What are the ages of the parents?

10. Can they afford surrogacy? Do they have the means to put enough money in escrow to meet the terms of the gestational surrogacy agreement?

11. If she needs medical insurance, will the intended parents pay for this?

12. How much communication does she hope for and expect during the journey? Will the intended parents be communicative with her?

13. Does she have thoughts on what kind of a relationship she may want or not want after the birth?

There are many other factors and considerations that go into the match, as each match is tailored to the individuals and couples involved. Again, the work of the surrogacy agency, specifically the recruiting and matching team, is to know the people they are working with and to propose matches that make sense considering the preferences that people have expressed.

Information in a Surrogate Profile

Here is an example of a surrogate's initial profile. This is the application that she completes. It does not have the psychological screening or background investigation results, which are provided to intended parents after they see this initial profile. Also, not all information is included here, as this is just a sample, although some answers are included to provide a flavor of how the profile sounds.

- name:
- address:
- date of birth:
- do you own or rent? *own*
- phone:
- height:
- weight:
- relationship status: *married*
- race:
- language(s) spoken at home: *English*
- pets: *no*
- Do you drink alcohol? *An occasional glass of wine with supper, one to two per month, never during pregnancy*
- Recently stop smoking? *No*
- Arrested? *No*
- High school diploma? *Yes*
- Did you attend a college or university? *Yes*

- Describe your household/living situation currently. Is it stable? *My husband and two kiddos. We live in our own home. We just sold our old home and moved in August. We love our new home.*
- How did you hear about Worldwide Surrogacy Specialists? *Already had one journey with WSS.*
- Employer name:
- Position held: *Registered nurse, staff education nurse*
- Describe what type of work you do and your schedule: *I oversee staff development and education/policies.*
- Length of time at current employer: *twelve years*
- Will your employer be flexible with your need to take time off for embryo transfers and medical appointments and court proceedings and for the birth of the child/children? *Yes*
- Are you receiving state assistance or Medicaid? *No*
- Relationship status: *Married*
- Name of spouse:
- Spouse's date of birth:
- Date of marriage:
- Briefly describe your relationship with your spouse/partner: *We have been together for nineteen years and married for sixteen. He is my "person." True partner. He supports me in all my crazy ventures.*
- Is your spouse/partner supportive of your interest in surrogacy and willing to undergo required testing? *Yes*
- Are you currently involved in a separation or divorce from your spouse/partner? *No*
- Is your spouse/partner employed? *Yes*
- Spouse/Partner employer name:
- Spouse/Partner position held: *information technology*
- Does your spouse/partner drive? *Yes*
- Does your spouse/partner smoke? *No*
- Any person in your house who smokes must do so outside the home and not in your car. Is this acceptable to you (if applicable)? *Yes*
- Has your spouse/partner ever been arrested? *No*
- Convicted of a crime? *No*
- Have you ever been a gestational surrogate? *Yes, delivered in May 2020. I was a patient of Dr. ________.*
- Have you ever been a traditional surrogate? *No*
- Briefly describe why you want to become a surrogate: *I loved my first journey so much. It was amazing to be so close to watching another family start. It was such an amazing experience for my whole family.*
- Provide three adjectives to describe yourself. *Loyal, loving, nonjudgmental*
- Do you exercise? *Yes*
- Briefly describe your diet (vegetarian, vegan, etc.): *I try to eat as clean as I can, but I live in Wisconsin, so I do love cheese. I limit processed and sugar-heavy foods when possible.*

- Are you willing to work with single father, single mother, gay couple (two dads), gay couple (two moms), heterosexual couple, international single parent or couple, interracial couple, couple with children, single parents or couples over the age of fifty, HIV+ clients?

  Note: Here the surrogate applicant will provide the agency with her preferences regarding the profile of intended parents she may be interested in. Also note that all the listed categories of parents have been matched and have had children through surrogacy, so this inquiry should not cause concern for intended parents

- How much communication do you expect or desire to have with the intended parents:
  - Before and during pregnancy: *I have had a very close relationship with my previous intended parents and welcome as much as these intended parents would like. Even if they want updates daily or multiple times per day. I would prefer daily texts vs. daily phone calls. I am fine with calls weekly or biweekly.*
  - After the baby(ies) are born: *Totally up to the parents! I still text/ message my former intended parents a couple of times per week but would be fine with less if that is what they want.*
- Carry twins? *No*
- Willing to do an amniocentesis and/or chorionic villus sampling (CVS)? *Yes*
- Are you willing to travel to your intended parents' IVF clinic? *Yes*
- What is the closest major airport to you?
- How can you reassure your intended parents you will not back out of your commitment to help them? *I am dedicated to this process 100 percent. I have been through IVF personally and again with my intended parents in my first journey. I know exactly what this entails, and I am 100 percent committed. I truly want to be involved in this and feel it is such an amazing experience. Until you decide to discontinue our journey together or you are holding your baby, I am on your team with all my dedication and heart.*
- What qualities are most important to you in intended parents? *Open-minded, dedicated, good communicators, and honest. This can be a long process, so these are qualities I feel make it easier.*
- Do you understand that you will not have custody of or legal rights to any child/children born because of your surrogate pregnancy? *Yes*
- When are you willing to start?
- If you know what you will request as base compensation, please enter an amount:
- If you have Skype/Facetime, please list your username(s):

Pregnancy History and Children

- First Pregnancy
  - Date of delivery: 04-26-2014
  - Months to conceive: one

- ○ Early delivery: *not applicable*
- ○ Number of weeks pregnant: *40.5*
- ○ Gender: *Male*
- ○ Birth weight: *7.2 lbs.*
- ○ Medication used: *IVF*
- ○ If multiples, how many?
- ○ Did you have problems with the delivery? *No*

- Second Pregnancy
  - ○ Date of delivery: *10-18-2016*
  - ○ Months to conceive: *one*
  - ○ Early delivery: *Not applicable*
  - ○ Number of weeks pregnant: *40.3*
  - ○ Gender: *female*
  - ○ Birth weight: *8.2 lbs.*
  - ○ Medication used: *IVF*
  - ○ If multiples, how many?
  - ○ Did you have problems with the delivery? *No*
- What are the ages of your children?
- Have you ever experienced any pregnancy complications, such as preterm labor, gestational diabetes, placenta previa, emergency cesarean, home monitoring? *No*
- Have you ever had a cesarean section? *No*
- Are you currently breastfeeding? *No*
- Do you currently have a sexually transmitted disease/infection? *No*
- Are you sexually active? *Yes*
- What form of birth control are you currently using? *Vasectomy*
- Do you have any preference as to an obstetrician? *No*
- Current OB/GYN name:
  - ○ Current OB/GYN phone number:
  - ○ Current OB/GYN address:
- Emergency contact name:
- Emergency contact number:
- Approximate date of last visit to the OB/GYN?
- Approximate date of last pap smear (if you know)?
- What were the results (e.g., normal):
- Do you have any issues that could come up in the psychological screening process that could disqualify you as a surrogate?
- Have you ever been on any antianxiety or antidepressant medication?
- Have you ever had any serious medical conditions/diseases?
- Are you currently under a physician's care?
- List all prescription and nonprescription medications you are currently taking, including the medication name, dose, and reason:

In addition to the information contained in the initial application as shown above, the surrogate will complete documentation, including a HIPAA privacy authorization form, to provide additional information to the surrogacy agency so that the agency team can investigate further, conduct additional screening, and obtain all the pregnancy-related medical records that will be reviewed by the IVF physician.

Stage 2: Legal and Medical

The second stage takes approximately three months, and it is the period from the match commitment to the embryo transfer. In the first part of this period, the gestational surrogacy contract is drafted, reviewed with legal counsel, and signed. As stated, the surrogate should have independent counsel outside the agency.

The intended parents may be represented by an agency lawyer if the agency has lawyers on staff and if jurisdictional issues permit—that is, if the lawyer is licensed to practice law in the state where the legal matters are taking place. If the intended parents require legal counsel outside the agency, they should be referred to competent legal counsel. Competent means that the lawyer specializes in assisted reproduction technology law (ART law).

It is worthwhile noting that some state laws have specific requirements as to the legal representation of the intended parents and the surrogate. For example, the New York Child Parent Security Act (CPSA), effective as of February 15, 2021, requires that the lawyers representing the intended parents and the surrogate not be affiliated with the surrogacy agency (surrogacy program, as it is referred to in the New York law). This adds to the emphasis on the legal complexity of gestational surrogacy. These specific requirements must be followed to satisfy the laws of the state and thereby ensure that the surrogacy agreement is enforceable and will lead to the establishment of parental rights for the intended parents. Any lawyers who take on the representation of intended parents and surrogates must be knowledgeable about the laws that will apply to their clients' cases and contracts and what must be done to comply with these laws—for example, which provisions must be contained in the gestational surrogacy contracts, which lawyers are eligible to represent the various parties, and what are the court procedures that are necessary for establishing legal parentage.

It usually takes a few weeks to a month to complete the drafting, review, and execution of the surrogacy agreement (gestational surrogacy contract). It may take longer depending on the lawyers involved, their obligations to other work they are doing, the negotiations, and the time it takes the parties to review the agreement and respond to their attorneys. Every case is different, but, for the most part, the period from the confirmation of the match between intended parents and surrogate and the embryo transfer will be approximately three months, including the time to draft, review, revise, and execute the gestational surrogacy agreement.

Stage 3: Pregnancy

The third stage of the journey is the pregnancy. By this time, the intended parents and the surrogate are communicating with each other, and they have most likely developed a warm and positive relationship. Surrogates are eager to involve the intended parents in all aspects of the pregnancy. Communication styles will vary, but surrogates understand that the intended parents are excited and nervous and that they want to know the details of how the surrogate is doing and feeling and how the pregnancy is developing. They will be communicating regularly by text, video chat, or email, and they may visit each other from time to time. The parents will be authorized to attend medical appointments and obtain medical records regarding the pregnancy. If they are not living near the surrogate, often the surrogate will video-chat with them during her prenatal appointments so that they can participate in this way.

Relationships between Surrogates and Intended Parents

A major benefit of using a qualified and experienced surrogacy agency is that the agency team will always be able to act as the liaison between the intended parents and the surrogate if there is ever a need for a facilitator to help with any issues that may arise. Another primary benefit is that when such an agency is managing and coordinating the surrogacy process, there is rarely ever any issue between parents and their surrogate. The rigorous and intensive screening of the surrogates and the counseling of the intended parents set the stage for a very warm, fulfilling journey for the intended parents and the surrogate as well as her family. If concerns arise, they will be resolved by the agency team and/or the lawyers and physicians. Here are some examples:

In one case, the intended father lived in Europe and the surrogate lived in Florida. He was concerned because she was not communicating with him enough. Her texts were sporadic, and she did not seem available for video chats. The surrogacy agency's case coordinator determined that the surrogate's cell phone was not functioning properly. The agency sent the surrogate to a cell service provider and paid for the surrogate to get a new cell phone. She was thrilled and the problem was solved!

In a more serious situation, a surrogate underwent a double embryo transfer and one of the embryos divided. A high-risk obstetrician recommended a reduction of the pregnancy from a triplet pregnancy to a twin pregnancy for the safety of the surrogate and to try to sustain a healthy twin pregnancy. In this case, the surrogate was having second thoughts about undergoing a selective reduction, although when she was screened, she agreed that she would undergo this procedure if requested. The surrogacy agency support team provided a great deal of support to the surrogate and to the intended parents. The team encouraged the surrogate to follow the recommendation of the high-risk physician, essentially for her own well-being, and she eventually did undergo the selective reduction medical procedure. The pregnancy continued and the twins were born healthy.

The reality is that surrogacy arrangements often involve people who are just getting to know each other. All people who are part of a surrogacy match have needs and desires and personal ideas about how they hope things will go. People also have busy lives. The intended parents most likely work and have the responsibilities of their everyday lives, and the surrogate has her work, family, and her own responsibilities in her everyday life. The more that people can step into the shoes of each other and have mutual respect and concern for each other, the better and more fulfilling the journey will be. Further, it is always important in almost all surrogacy arrangements to have a team of professionals to provide support, knowledge, and understanding.

The intended parents will be participating with the surrogate in the pregnancy to the extent they are able. Many parents live outside the United States, and their involvement will be by video chats, texting, email, and phone. Other parents may be able to attend prenatal examinations and ultrasounds, and they will have the authorization to do this. Also, the surrogate enjoys sharing these aspects of the pregnancy with the intended parents.

Establishing Legal Parentage

In addition to the importance of a healthy pregnancy, the well-being of the surrogate, and making sure the intended parents have all of the information they need and want, the most important aspect of the journey during the pregnancy is establishing the legal parentage of the intended parents. They want to know that their baby will be placed in their arms at the time of the birth. They need legal safety and security, which will in turn provide emotional security.

The legal procedures will be conducted by a lawyer in the state where the birth will take place, which is most likely where the surrogate resides. The work of the agency is to make sure that the legal procedures are initiated and that they are being conducted in a timely manner and efficiently to make sure the parents are legally all set for the birth of their baby. The agency lawyer or case manager must keep in contact with the lawyer conducting the legal procedures to obtain the parents' order of legal parentage. This is done as a system of checks so that there is never a time that a pre-birth order would slip through the cracks and not get done in time for the birth. Further, if it is a state with a post-birth legal process to establish parentage, the lawyers should be initiating the process before the birth so that the process is ready to go as soon as possible at the time of the birth.

Making sure to obtain the order of legal parentage (prebirth or post-birth order) is essential to the legal security of the parents and the newborn at the hospital when the birth occurs. It will ensure that the hospital staff clearly recognizes the intended parents as the legal parents, and it will further ensure that the baby is placed with and cared for by her or his legal parents. Also, in the event of any medical complications involving the newborn, the parents will have the necessary authority to make medical decisions for their infant.

In the hands of knowledgeable and experienced attorneys, the intended parents will have unambiguous legal authority for their newborn. Although the laws and procedures differ from state to state, there are many jurisdictions (states) in the United States that provide a clear path to establishing the legal parentage of the intended parents prior to the birth.

The law that will be applicable will be the law of the state where the delivery and birth are to occur. The intended parents will need a lawyer experienced in surrogacy law in the state that is the place of birth. This lawyer will know the law and the legal procedures necessary to accomplish the prebirth or post-birth order (PBO) of legal parentage.

Most US states that have favorable surrogacy laws allow the establishment of legal parentage before the birth (prebirth order). However, some states have procedures wherein the order of legal parentage is issued shortly after the birth. Usually, the lawyers will begin the process of establishing legal parentage so they can demonstrate to the hospital where the birth will occur that the intended parents are, in fact, the soon-to-be legal parents and that they and their surrogate agree that the baby belongs to the intended parents.

Some international intended parents, depending on what countries they are from, may need a post-birth order instead of a prebirth order because they may need a birth certificate showing the surrogate listed as the mother. This may be necessary to follow through with the intended parent's home country requirements to establish the citizenship of their baby in their home country. When this is necessary, there may then be a post-birth order or a second-parent adoption to assist the couple in naming both intended parents on a replacement or amended birth certificate.

It is essential that international intended parents consult with an experienced lawyer in their home country before beginning the surrogacy process so that they and their US lawyers know these requirements before the match is made with the surrogate. In this way, the US team can make sure the intended parents are matched in a state where the necessary legal procedures are possible. For example, in the United Kingdom, when parents return home, they must apply for and obtain a UK parental order so they will be recognized as the child's legal parents in the United Kingdom. There are deadlines for making the application, and there are documentation requirements. The documentation can be organized and collected during the surrogacy journey in the United States. Then, a knowledgeable surrogacy attorney or surrogacy agency in the United States will assist in the collection of the required documents for the UK parental order application.

For German intended parents, it may be necessary to include certain provisions in the gestational surrogacy agreement with the surrogate to note that the surrogate will agree to attend a meeting at the German Consulate in the United States. The US order establishing the parental rights of the German intended parents and relieving the surrogate of any parental obligations or rights is necessary, but it is not enough for the German intended parents to establish their legal parentage and the citizenship of their child in Germany. An additional step, to attend the German Consulate, where additional documents will be executed, is necessary.

In other countries outside the US, there may be requirements such as those mentioned above. This is why it is critical for international intended parents to obtain legal advice about their home country laws and procedures to bring their newborn home.

Intended Parents Attending the Birth

Almost all intended parents may be present in the birthing room when their babies are born. The surrogacy agreement will incorporate a provision wherein the gestational carrier states that the intended parents are authorized to be present for the birth. There may also be qualifying language to say that if the medical team allows only one person to attend the birth, the surrogate will be able to select the support person she wants in the room for her. However, it is always her intention and desire to have the intended parents witness the birth of their baby.

One reason for a limitation would be, for example, if there are medical complications and the surrogate would want her spouse or other support person with her. Also, if there is a medical emergency, the medical team will most likely limit who can be present and maybe even disallow anyone from being in attendance except the nurses and physicians.

Another complexity may be the fact that the intended parents are traveling to the hospital from abroad or from a distant location within the United States. This may cause such a delay that the intended parents will not be at the birth. Usually, however, even when parents must travel, there is enough planning and preparation time for them to arrive in time for the birth. It is only when the surrogate has a premature birth (rare in cases of singleton pregnancies) or when she goes into labor prior to the planned due date, although not so early as to be deemed a premature birth, that the intended parents may not arrive in time for the birth.

The foundational premise is that the intended parents are the legal parents prior to the birth by way of the prebirth order of legal parentage obtained prior to the birth by the parties' lawyers or by way of the surrogacy agreement and the preparations to do a post-birth order. In this way, there is no surprise or concern by the hospital staff and medical team regarding the expectation that the intended parents will be allowed in the birthing room at the hospital to witness the birth of their baby and that they will assume parental obligations and rights for their baby.

Often, the hospital will provide a private room, hospital space permitting, for the intended parents to have private bonding time with their newborn.

11

Potential Losses, Frustrations, and Delays During the Journey

The medical and legal risks of gestational surrogacy in the United States can be greatly minimized. Medical technology has advanced to a degree that pregnancy rates are high and the legal risks, when the parties are represented by attorneys who specialize in assisted reproduction technology law, may be reduced to virtually no risk.

However, the one area of risk that cannot be controlled is where mother nature is in control. Unwanted outcomes may occur along the surrogacy journey, causing emotional losses and frustrations for intended parents and surrogates. These occurrences may include the following:

- There may be a failed embryo transfer. The surrogate travels to the medical clinic for the embryo transfer, a much hoped for and exciting experience for everyone, but the transfer does not result in a pregnancy. The parties must regroup and plan for the next embryo transfer.
- There may be more than one failed embryo transfer, and if there are as many as three failed transfers, the IVF physician may recommend that the intended parents be matched with another surrogate. This is emotionally disappointing and frustrating. Also, the parents and the surrogate have most likely become close and now they must also manage the loss of this relationship.
- A pregnant surrogate may have a miscarriage. This is a great emotional loss for everyone and requires support from the medical and agency team. Usually, miscarriages happen early in the pregnancy, and therefore, most likely, the surrogate can try another embryo transfer if the doctor approves and if everyone wants to try again.
- The surrogate may not physiologically respond to the medications she takes to prepare her uterine lining for the embryo transfer. If this occurs, the IVF doctor will stop the medications and wait for the surrogate's next cycle and then restart the medications. If she again does not respond and

her uterine lining does not develop optimally for the embryo transfer, she will no longer be qualified to be a surrogate and the intended parents will have to be rematched with another surrogate. This will also cause disappointment, frustration, and delay.

- Occasionally, a surrogate will be unable to continue with the match because of personal reasons. (Of course, this would be before there is a pregnancy.) For example, she may have to relocate, or there may be a serious illness affecting someone in her immediate family, or a death in her immediate family, which could prevent her from continuing the surrogacy journey.

Resilience is a key ingredient for intended parents and surrogates. This quality is important to overcome hardships and obstacles that may occur during the surrogacy process. If intended parents and surrogates get support from the agency team, from the medical team, and perhaps, even counseling, they will be able to continue their path to having a child or children through surrogacy.

12

The Gestational Surrogacy Agreement

The agreement[38] between the intended parents and the surrogate, and the surrogate's spouse if she is married (gestational surrogacy agreement), is a lengthy document that expresses the parties'[39] rights and obligations during the surrogacy journey. These rights and obligations are specific to the legal relationship between the parties and their intentions as to how the journey will go and what they agree they will do under certain circumstances.

A primary goal in surrogacy is that there should be such rigorous and thorough preparation in matching the parties and assisting them through the drafting and execution of their agreement that there will be virtually no possibility of a contractual dispute. First, the agreement should be brought under the law of a state in the United States where it would be enforceable. Further, surrogacy is so unique in terms of legal agreements that all caution and clarity must be exercised to avoid any possibility for breach-of-contract claims.

Therefore, the gestational surrogacy agreement (contract) is a complex and detailed agreement with many provisions that will set forth the parties' intentions for their relationship during the surrogacy journey as well as their rights and obligations. Here is a list of topics that will be covered in the agreement:

- The names and addresses of all parties to the agreement.
- The gestational carrier will state that she is healthy; that to the best of her knowledge she is capable of bearing a child without unreasonable risk to herself or to any resulting child, physically or mentally; and that to the best of her knowledge she has no physical or genetic illnesses, abnormalities,

---

38. The agreement between the intended parents and their surrogate goes by various names. These include gestational carrier agreement, gestational carrier contract, gestational surrogacy agreement, gestational surrogacy contract, surrogacy agreement, and surrogacy contract. These terms are interchangeable, but in any scenario, there should be consistency. For purposes herein, we will use the term *agreement*.

39. *Parties* is an inclusive term that refers to all persons or entities who are or will be the signers to the agreement.

or traits that are known to adversely affect her own health or the health of any child that she will gestate and give birth to.

- The gestational carrier will state whether she is married or unmarried. If married, she will state that she will remain married during the surrogacy journey and that her spouse is supportive of her endeavor to carry a pregnancy as a gestational carrier; that she has had at least one pregnancy and has previously experienced at least one live birth; and that she agrees to promptly inform the intended parents of changes in her circumstances, such as health, residence, employment, and insurance.
- The parties will agree on the embryo transfer, how the embryos are created, where the embryo transfer will take place, that the surrogate will undergo the embryo transfer procedure when the IVF physician schedules it, and how many embryos transfers she will agree to undergo (usually three).
- The surrogate will state that she understands and acknowledges that she is giving birth to a child for whom the intended parents will have legal parental rights and custody.
- The surrogate and her spouse will agree to take all necessary legal steps including attending court, if necessary, to have the intended parents named as the custodial and legal parents, to have the intended parents named as the legal parents on the child's birth certificate, and to remove the surrogate's name from the child's birth certificate (if necessary).
- The surrogate will agree that, at the time of the birth, she will take no actions to bond in any way with the child, including holding the child, unless such action is with the consent and knowledge of the intended parents. Usually, the intended parents and the surrogate spend time together at the hospital with the baby after the birth.; and that if the intended parents must travel far for the birth, they will make diligent efforts to be present at the hospital for the birth of the child and will take full custody and responsibility immediately upon birth of the child.
- There is a statement to the effect that the intended parents may attend any or all prenatal medical examinations, that they may be present in the birthing room to witness the birth of their child, and that the surrogate will sign proper medical authorizations to allow this.
- The surrogate and her spouse will agree to follow the IVF physician's instructions before and after the embryo transfer and not engage in sexual relations to make sure the pregnancy is the result of the embryo transfer, and that the surrogate will follow the IVF physician's instructions regarding her level of activity following the embryo transfer.
- The surrogate will assume all the risks of the pregnancy and releases the intended parents from liability except for obligations under the agreement.
- The surrogate will agree to adhere to all medical instructions given to her by the physician performing the embryo transfer and all other physicians

who may become involved in the medical procedures related to the surrogacy.

- The surrogate will represent that all the information and medical history she provided is true and accurate.
- Medical insurance matters will be addressed, including what health insurance policy will cover the surrogate pregnancy and who will pay for it; what happens if the health insurance policy is canceled; and whether the surrogate has her own medical insurance, it will cover the surrogate pregnancy.
- The intended parents will represent that they are responsible for all medical bills not covered by the health insurance policy, including copays, deductibles, and other portions of the medical bills that are not covered by the insurance.
- The intended parents will represent that they will pay for the medical bills of their newborn.
- The surrogate, her spouse, and the intended parents will represent that they are free from diseases that could cause harm either to the fetus or to the surrogate.
- The surrogate will agree to submit to periodic testing for alcohol, nicotine, and drugs, as requested by any treating physician or the intended parents.
- The surrogate will agree to make the necessary changes to her lifestyle to ensure a healthy pregnancy, to minimize the risks to her own well-being, and to minimize risks of harm to the unborn child, including requesting any temporary changes in her present employment situation necessary to remove her from the known presence of chemicals and conditions considered by any federal or state occupational safety agency, or by the IVF physician or treating obstetrician, to be harmful to pregnant women.
- The surrogate will agree to avoid contact with environmental risk factors to pregnancy, including animal feces, kitty litter, and contact with animals that may pose a threat to the pregnancy; she will not handle or be unreasonably exposed to chemical cleansers, pesticides, and paint fumes. During her pregnancy, the surrogate agrees to avoid high-impact sports and high-risk activities. The surrogate agrees that she will not consume raw, smoked, or undercooked fish and meat (including but not limited to sushi, ceviche, carpaccio), raw or partially cooked eggs (including but not limited to mousse, unprocessed Caesar dressing, unprocessed mayonnaise), mold-ripened soft cheese (including but not limited to brie, camembert, blue cheese, and gorgonzola), unpasteurized dairy products, and any fruits and vegetables that she knows are unwashed. The surrogate will agree to abstain from any high-risk sexual conduct that may result in contraction of a sexually transmitted disease by the surrogate or any unborn child; to abstain from the legal or illegal and potentially harmful use of chemicals, including, but not limited to, alcohol, nicotine, caffeine (except in permissible amounts as recommended by the IVF physician or treating obstetrician), prescription medication (unless necessary and prescribed or approved by the treating obstetrician or treating IVF physician for the health of the gestational carrier);

to abstain from any and all recreational or street drugs whether legal or illegal; to abstain from over-the-counter drugs and medications unless they can be safely taken by a pregnant woman (and they are prescribed or approved by the treating obstetrician or treating IVF physician); and to avoid using health and beauty products (including but not limited to hair dye) that pose a risk to a pregnant woman and or the unborn child carried by the pregnant woman. When in doubt about a particular substance or conduct, the surrogate agrees that she will discuss the use of the substance or the conduct in question with her treating physician or the treating IVF physician, and she will abide by the physician's recommendation.

- The surrogate's spouse represents that he is in support of his wife becoming pregnant as a surrogate and he agrees to submit to the blood testing and to comply with his contractual obligations under the agreement.
- All parties represent that they will undergo medical testing for syphilis, gonorrhea, acquired immune deficiency syndrome (AIDS), and other sexually transmitted diseases and all tests required by the IVF clinic performing the embryo transfer, and that the results of those tests will be available for review by the intended parents' chosen physicians.
- Provisions for whether the pregnancy will be terminated if there is a severe fetal abnormality will be addressed in the agreement.
- Provisions for whether there will be a selective reduction if there is a severe fetal abnormality with one of the fetuses will be addressed in the agreement.
- The surrogate will agree to undergo medically necessary testing, such as amniocentesis, fetal DNA blood test, and/or other tests designed to detect genetic and congenital defects.
- The surrogate will agree to make diligent efforts and take all reasonable steps to give birth to any child carried pursuant to this agreement in the state where she resides due to the importance of the intended parents accessing the laws of this state to establish their legal parentage.
- There will be a provision for DNA testing of the baby and the surrogate and her spouse to be sure that the intended parents are the genetic parents of the baby.
- The intended parents will agree to release the surrogate and her spouse from liability for pregnancy complications and birth defects, providing the surrogate is not in breach of the agreement.
- There will be a provision in which all parties will acknowledge that all decisions related to the newborn child(ren) immediately upon the birth and at all times after the birth will be made by the intended parents.
- There will be detailed provisions related to the compensation that the surrogate will receive and the expenses that the intended parents will pay or reimburse:
  - travel expenses
  - medical bills
  - maternity clothing

- ◦ monthly allowance
- ◦ housekeeping
- ◦ childcare
- ◦ surrogate's lost wages
- ◦ surrogate's spouse's lost wages
- ◦ legal expenses
- ◦ payments to the surrogate for undergoing invasive medical procedures and tests
- ◦ potential payments for loss of reproductive organs
- ◦ potential payments for breast milk
- ◦ allowance for counseling
- ◦ base compensation
- ◦ additional base compensation for multiple pregnancy
- breach of contract provisions and potential remedies for breach of contract.
- provision for life insurance for the surrogate to be paid for by the intended parents.
- provisions for when and why the agreement may be terminated.
- intended parents' designation of guardian(s) for their newborn.
- confidentiality provisions
- the parties' acknowledgment that they have had the benefit of independent legal counsel.
- provisions for the funding of the intended parents' escrow account.
- which US state's law will govern the agreement.

The gestational carrier agreements must be reviewed for each party by independent legal counsel. There will be many details in the agreement to define and provide substance for the outline of contract provisions listed above. Further, the agreement will go back and forth between the lawyers to reach a final draft of the agreement with which all parties are satisfied. Although it is a lengthy and detailed document, there are many standard, expected provisions. For example, the compensation terms should have been disclosed and discussed with each party prior to getting to the contract review stage. This is good practice to avoid negotiations that may create awkwardness or discomfort between the parties. When the match is being made between intended parents and surrogate, the important provisions covering compensation, insurance, potential termination of pregnancy, medical process, and state of birth will have already been settled before the parties get to the contract stage.

13

The Laws of Gestational Surrogacy

Laws, Lawyers, and Legal Procedure

When it comes to legal matters in gestational surrogacy, one of the most important ingredients for a smooth journey is choosing the right lawyer to represent the intended parents and a separate lawyer to represent the surrogate. Through an organization called the Academy of Adoption and Assisted Reproduction Attorneys (AAAA),[40] intended parents and surrogates or other professionals and individuals working within the field of assisted reproduction may find attorneys competent in handling surrogacy matters. By visiting the website or doing other research to find attorneys who specialize in assisted reproduction technology law (ART law), it is possible to find lawyers who are competent in the areas of surrogacy law and surrogacy legal procedure.

Many intended parents come from countries other than the United States to have their babies through surrogacy in the United States. There are very good reasons for this. In the United States, surrogacy is legally authorized in that the intended parents will have laws to protect their parental rights. As discussed, the intended parents will become the legal parents of their baby prior to the birth in almost all cases. There are a few states where the process to confirm legal parentage is commenced prior to the birth and finalized immediately after the birth. These legal procedures will be discussed with the intended parents at the time they are matched with their surrogate. Whatever the procedures to establish legal parentage are, the professional team will make sure that, at the time of the birth, there will be absolutely no question that the intended parents are the legal parents of the baby. The parents will take responsibility for their baby immediately upon the birth. There is no waiting period and no question about this.

Further, the intended parents will have the protection of a legally enforceable gestational surrogacy agreement. Although the gestational surrogates are clear with their intentions and obligations to deliver the baby for the intended

---

40. Academy of Adoption and Assisted Reproduction Attorneys, https://adoptionart.org/.

parents, when the intended parents express the concern about whether the surrogate will relinquish the baby to the parents, there are very clear safeguards: (1) the surrogate is rigorously screened by a mental health provider regarding this aspect of her obligations; and (2) the surrogacy contract as well as the laws and the legal procedures in the state where the birth will take place provide legal protection against this occurrence.

Other reasons for going through gestational surrogacy in the United States include the medical advancements in technology and cryopreservation, the favorable laws regarding the intended parents' rights when it comes to egg and sperm donation, and the clear and unambiguous ethical framework within which gestational surrogacy is conducted in the United States.

Enforcement of Gestational Surrogacy Agreements

When we discuss the concept of legal safety in gestational surrogacy, what we are really talking about is the basic premise that the intended parents will be named as the legal parents of the baby to be born because of the assisted reproduction process and the embryo transfer by which the gestational surrogate becomes pregnant. A key element in establishing legal security is the fact that a gestational surrogacy agreement will be valid and enforceable in the state where the birth takes place.

The attorneys representing the intended parents and the surrogate must advise the parties regarding these legal matters and make sure that the parties are entering into their surrogacy agreement in a state in the United States, where, in the unlikely event of a dispute, the agreement will be reviewed by a court of competent jurisdiction and, if drafted and executed properly, will be enforced. Further, in the event of a dispute regarding the agreement, the party who needs to enforce the agreement will have rights and available legal processes to do so in the state where the birth is to take place.

It is the responsibility of the attorneys to draft the agreement properly under the laws that are to govern the agreement. For example, in Connecticut, a gestational surrogacy agreement must be witnessed and notarized. This is a statutory requirement and, therefore, the attorneys must be sure to have the agreement executed in accordance with Connecticut law requirements for gestational surrogacy agreements.

Although these elements of contract law and procedure are critical, there is another important concept to cover when discussing how to create legal safety for the parties. And that is the screening of the parties as well as the discussions between the lawyers and their clients while drafting and negotiating the surrogacy agreement.

To create a stable match between intended parents and their surrogate, and to reduce legal risk to virtually none, the professionals assisting with the match must take great care to ensure that thorough screening is done so that all parties have clear expectations of their rights and obligations as they go through the surrogacy journey together. Reputable surrogacy agencies and medical clinics as well as knowledgeable attorneys will prepare and advise their clients and patients on how to have a positive and loving surrogacy journey in this most important endeavor to bring a newborn baby into the world.

For an example of a bad case where people suffered as a result of not going ahead with a competent professional team who would have greatly helped in reducing the risks of heart-wrenching outcomes, see the article below by Attorney Ellen Trachman:

Extreme Surrogacy Nightmare Heads to Iowa Supreme Court: A Cautionary Tale[41]

by Ellen Trachman, June 28, 2017

The latest surrogacy-gone-wrong case is the stuff of every intended parent's nightmare. The Montovers—a couple in Iowa who married later in life—nevertheless wished to have a child together. Unable to conceive and carry on their own, they turned to an anonymous egg donor and, separately, a gestational carrier (what we all know as a surrogate). Unfortunately, what followed may be one of the worst cases out there on a surrogacy relationship breaking down. And there are plenty of lessons to go around.

Do Not Use Craigslist To Have A Baby. The Montovers chose to forgo using an agency. Instead, they hoped to find someone on their own. They posted an ad for a surrogate on Craigslist (among other sites) and one woman reached out to them, offering to take them up on their offer. She asked the Montovers to pay for her to go through an IVF cycle, at the same clinic and cost of their own cycle—a cost of $13,000. The Montovers accepted the surrogate's offer and entered into a gestational carrier agreement with her.

Shortly after the embryo transfer, the Montovers and the surrogate attended the 8-week ultrasound together. They received the good news! At least one fetus was thriving, and there was even a possibility that the surrogate was carrying two babies. Amazingly, things seemed like they might work out at first. But you know that the story wouldn't be in this column if everything had just gone as planned.

Unfortunately, the surrogate increased her request for compensation from $13,000 to $30,000. That's a hefty jump! Worse, the surrogate indicated that she may abort the pregnancy, or give the children away if the Montovers did not comply with her demand for more money. Obviously, the relationship between the parties quickly fell apart, and the Montovers never saw another ultrasound.

As an aside, I must point out that a disproportionate number of the baby-making tragedies I see start the same way . . . with Craigslist. By all means, find your apartment or used furniture on Craigslist. You can get some great

---

41. Ellen Trachman, "Extreme Surrogacy Nightmare Heads to Iowa Supreme Court: A Cautionary Tale," Above the Law, June 28, 2017, https://abovethelaw.com/2017/06/extreme-surrogacy-nightmare-heads-to-iowa-supreme-court/.

deals! But please, refrain from using the site when it comes to procreating. Well, at least the type of procreation involving non-traditional methods.

Allegations of Racism. The surrogate now contends that the Montovers made racists remarks to her and her sister-in-law in the course of their relationship. She even says that they used the "N" word. The Montovers are Caucasian, while the surrogate is African American. According to court documents, the surrogate concluded that she could not let the babies (spoiler alert, the surrogate was, indeed, carrying twins) be raised by racists. She cut off contact with the Montovers and determined that she would keep the babies for herself.

Lack of Communication. The surrogate went into labor prematurely. At this point, having cut off all contact, she did not inform the Montovers of the birth of the babies. Nor did she inform the Montovers when one of the babies, little Baby K, tragically died eight days after birth. The surrogate even made the decision to have Baby K's remains cremated. The Montovers noted that cremation would not have been their wish for their baby's remains. The other twin, Baby H, survived and is thriving. But custody and parentage is at the heart of this legal battle.

The Montovers brought a legal action to seek to enforce the contract; and immediately after learning of Baby H's birth and survival, amended to request custody. The trial court ruled in their favor and enforced the surrogacy agreement giving the Montovers parental rights. But the surrogate appealed directly to the Iowa Supreme Court (because in Iowa you can skip those pesky intermediary courts—although the Supreme Court then determines what to hear itself and what to send to the Court of Appeals).

The Surrogate's Attorney May Sound Familiar. Among the surrogate's attorneys, a familiar name pops up among assisted reproductive technology (ART) law practitioners: Harold Cassidy. Cassidy is the attorney who represented the surrogate in the famous Baby M case. That 1987 case involved a "traditional" surrogacy in New Jersey, where the surrogate changed her mind about the arrangement and kidnapped the baby.

Cassidy also represented the surrogate in the California triplets case I wrote about last year. There, a surrogate fought for parental rights of the triplets she carried based on the intended father's request to reduce the pregnancy from three fetuses to two. The surrogate lost that case, and the intended father kept the triplets. Cassidy has repeatedly argued before courts that enforcing surrogacy agreements over the objections of the birth mother surrogate violates the US Constitution.

Is Surrogacy Unconstitutional? Cassidy argues that a court's enforcement of a surrogacy contract violates the Fourteenth Amendment rights of the surrogate, and of the surrogate-born child. He argues that the violation is three-fold: (1) that the baby has a fundamental liberty interest in a parent-child relationship with the surrogate; (2) the baby has a fundamental liberty interest in being free from commodification; and (3) the surrogate has a fundamental liberty interest in not being exploited.

The Iowan lower court summarily dismissed each of these contentions, noting that (1) since the surrogate is not the rightful, legal parent of the child, there is no parent-child relationship between the surrogate and child to protect; (2) the baby is not being commodified by a surrogacy arrangement; and (3) the surrogate is not being exploited—she was a willful and free participant in the arrangement to offer her services to help others have a child.

The attorneys for the Montovers—Philip J. De Koster and Casey Rigdon—are optimistic about the pending Iowa Supreme Court appeal. They believe gestational surrogacy contracts are, indeed, enforceable under Iowa law and the US Constitution and believe that the asserted constitutional challenges are insufficient to void such a contract.

With any luck, the Montovers will soon be raising their daughter in peace. And hopefully, prospective parents can avoid the same tragedy, and learn a few things from the Montovers' mistakes. Unfortunately, other intended parents must keep their fingers crossed that they never show up on Cassidy's anti-surrogacy-crusading radar.

In the Crystal Kelley case, discussed in chapter 6, "Thoughts and Considerations for Gestational Surrogates," the intended parents wanted to terminate the pregnancy, but the surrogate, Crystal Kelley, was against termination. She fled Connecticut and relocated to Michigan, where the surrogacy agreement could not legally be enforced. She gave birth to the baby, who required numerous surgeries and who was eventually adopted by a couple who had adopted other special-needs children. Attorney Melissa Brisman, in her blog post covering an interview with CNN.com, "How to Keep Your Surrogacy Conflict Free,"[42] Brisman explains what happened in the Crystal Kelley case, and what could have been done to avoid the nightmarish circumstances that this case presents:

How to Keep Your Surrogacy Conflict Free
CNN.com
March 7, 2013

By Elizabeth Cohen, Senior Medical Correspondent

When Crystal Kelley agreed to carry someone else's baby, she didn't, in her words, "dot every *i* and cross every *t*."

---

42. Elizabeth Cohen, "How to Keep Your Surrogacy Conflict Free," interview with Melissa Brisman, CNN, posted on Melissa B. Brisman, Esq., blog, https://www.reproductivelawyer.com/2013/03/how-to-keep-your-surrogacy-conflict-free/.

That turned her surrogacy dream into a nightmare.

Surrogacy has become an increasingly popular way of having a baby. In 2010 there were 1,448 babies born to surrogates, up from 738 babies in 2004, according to the Society for Assisted Reproductive Technologies. Celebrities such as Nicole Kidman, Sarah Jessica Parker and Giuliana Rancic have helped increase awareness by using a surrogate. In a surrogacy arrangement, a woman agrees to carry someone else's baby for a fee.... The egg and sperm can come from the couple who hire the surrogate, or a donor egg or sperm are used.

Sometimes parents know their surrogate—she might be a sister or a friend. Other times the parents meet the surrogate through an agency.

Surrogates and intended parents must be well matched, says Melissa Brisman, who practices reproductive law in New Jersey and runs a surrogacy agency.

For example, if parents feel strongly that they would terminate the pregnancy if a fetal abnormality were found, they shouldn't be matched with a surrogate who is adamantly opposed to abortion.

"You want to flesh out those issues and make sure you're on the same page," Brisman says.

Serious conflicts between surrogates and intended parents are relatively rare; Brisman estimates that out of thousands of surrogate pregnancies, only about a dozen have ended up in court.

But when problems do arise, as in Kelley's case, the ending can be disastrous. Kelley says she assumed the parents were, like her, against abortion because the mother said her frozen embryos were her "babies" and she had to give them a chance at life. But when the fetus Kelley was carrying turned out to have birth defects, the parents wanted to abort, and she didn't.

Making assumptions when going into a surrogacy arrangement is not a good idea, says Brisman, a founding member of the Academy of Adoption and Assisted Reproduction Technology Attorneys.

Here are her tips for having a surrogacy arrangement with a happy ending.

1. Each side should have an attorney

The surrogate and the intended parents should each have their own lawyer to review the contract.

2. Understand the limits of the contract

Even if the surrogate signs a contract agreeing to abortion if there's a fetal abnormality, she can later change her mind. "You can't force her to have an abortion," Brisman says.

3. Agree on prenatal testing

Sometimes intended parents want an amniocentesis but the surrogate doesn't want the test, which would involve having a needle stuck in her stomach. The two sides should come to an agreement before the pregnancy takes place.

4. Have a full psychological evaluation

In Brisman's practice, the surrogate and intended parents sit together for five or six hours to have a full discussion on many issues, including abortion. Kelley said the intended parents weren't present at her evaluation, which was done over the telephone. The subject of abortion never came up, she added. She said the evaluation was done by [a counselor] who work[ed] at . . . the agency that arranged the surrogacy. That's a problem, Brisman says. A person who works for the agency stands to benefit financially if the surrogacy goes through and might be tempted to overlook potential conflicts that could kill the deal. CNN contacted [the agency], and a woman . . . answered the phone. "You have to understand something—there is a privacy that exists and that's the end of the story," she said and then hung up.

5. Understand the relationship after birth

Will the surrogate pump breast milk for the baby? Will the parents send photos of the baby as he or she grows up? Can the surrogate contact the parents for updates? All these questions should be worked out beforehand, Brisman says.

Prebirth and Post-birth Orders of Legal Parentage

The legal process to establish the legal parentage of the intended parents in a gestational surrogacy arrangement can take various forms. There are different laws and procedures in each US state where surrogacy is permitted.

In surrogacy, legal parentage is most often established prior to the birth of the baby. These orders or judgments are referred to as prebirth orders. This means that the legal parentage of the intended parents is established prior to the birth of their baby. In such cases, the intended parents actually and legally are the legal parents of the baby at the moment of birth. All medical providers as well as the surrogate, her spouse, and her family and anyone else involved in the process will recognize the intended parents as the legal parents.

This is crucial information for the hospital staff at the time of birth so that the intended parents are legally authorized to take custody of the newborn baby and to make all decisions regarding the baby's care. There will be no question at the hospital regarding the intended parents' rights and obligations regarding the baby's medical care and all the decisions to be made on behalf of the baby. Further, there will be no question that the intended parents will have private time with their baby and that the baby will be discharged to their care and control.

Another procedural form to establish the legal parentage of the intended parents is by way of a post-birth order. This means that the legal parentage is established after the baby is born. While this is acceptable, it is not as ideal as the prebirth order. In states where a post-birth order is the path to legal parentage, arrangements must be made, and additional legal documents drafted to ensure that the intended parents have the necessary authority to care for and make decisions for their baby at the time of birth.

When a post-birth order is the way parentage is established, the surrogate may be considered the legal mother at the time of birth. She will have to sign documentation to authorize the intended parents to have authority for the baby. Such documentation may be a power of attorney or a designation of guardian. There should be a competent surrogacy attorney overseeing the legal process before the birth so that the intended parents' legal parental status is accomplished as soon as possible after the birth.

A power of attorney is a simple document that can be drafted by a lawyer and signed by the surrogate. This document is often used in estate planning or health-care legal matters, as it is a method by which a person gives authority to another person to act on his or her behalf. The post-birth order must be obtained for the intended parents to gain their status as legal parents of their newborn baby. In jurisdictions, such as Florida and other states, the post-birth order process is legally safe and routinely done.

One reason a post-birth order may be necessary is if the baby is born prematurely and the prebirth order has not yet been obtained. This is rare since prebirth-order legal procedures are usually started in ample time prior to a birth.

In the past, there was another reason that some intended parents wanted a post-birth order. This was around insurance needs. Although this has always been a topic of controversy among lawyers in the United States, there was a period of time when international intended parents wanted to be able to use the surrogate's medical insurance for their baby. The idea was that if the surrogate was still the legal mother at the time of birth, the baby might be legally covered by the surrogate's health insurance. Some lawyers would say this is acceptable because the surrogate is the legal mother at the time of birth and her name would be designated on the child's birth certificate. The argument follows that since the insurance policy is a contract of insurance and if the surrogate is the legal mother, then she could add the baby as her dependent newborn and have his or her medical expenses at birth covered by the insurance.

However, a different argument was that the use of the surrogate's insurance for the newborn was not a legitimate use of the insurance and not a legally acceptable method by which to insure the baby because the surrogate mother was never intended to be the legal mother of the baby. In fact, there was an executed surrogacy agreement stating that the intended parents were to become the legal parents and that the surrogate would not be the legal parent of the baby. The baby was never actually a dependent of the surrogate since, even in the post-birth order scenario, the intended parents took custody of the baby and acted as the baby's parents from the moment of birth.

A post-birth order might be preferred if the intended parents are from another country where they need this legal mechanism to establish their legal rights in their home country. For example, in some countries, it is necessary to show that the surrogate is on the initial birth certificate. The purpose is to demonstrate to international authorities the legal process transferring the parental rights to the intended parents.

A Word on Second-Parent[43] Adoptions

A second-parent adoption, also known as a confirmatory adoption or co-parent adoption, is a legal proceeding whereby a person acting as a parent of a child becomes the legal parent for that child through an adoption process. This occurs when a couple is either married (stepparent adoption) or unmarried (second-parent adoption) and one of the parents is the legal parent of the child and desires to establish his or her spouse or partner to also become a legal parent of the child.

When couples are married and have a baby naturally (i.e., a woman in the couple gives birth), even if one parent is not genetically related to the baby, that parent is the presumed parent of the baby by virtue of the marriage to the birth parent. When this occurs, the birth certificate will include the name of the spouse of the birth parent. This is called marital presumption. For example, if a married, heterosexual woman gives birth to a baby whom she conceived with a man other than her spouse, her spouse will still be the presumed parent of the baby. The exception or rebuttal to this presumption occurs if the mother and genetic father execute a voluntary acknowledgment of parentage, or if there is a paternity proceeding. If this is done, the biological/genetic father will be named on the child's birth certificate, not the spouse.

With marriage equality for same-sex couples having become the law of the United States, this marital presumption now extends to same-sex couples. For a married lesbian couple, the wife of a birth mother is the presumed legal parent of the child born to the birth mother. The problem with this legal status is that this legal presumption may be rebutted (in law, this is called a rebuttable presumption). In the event gay marriage rights are dissolved, the presumption may become null and void. For this reason, the second parent is advised to do a confirmatory adoption (a/k/a second-parent adoption or co-parent adoption) of her legal rights.

For a gay male couple, the issues are similar but slightly different. If a married gay male couple has a child through gestational surrogacy, using the sperm of one of the partners in that marriage, the sperm-contributing partner

---

43. Second-Parent adoption is a term that refers to the adoption of a baby by her or his co-parent (the individual parent who is part of a couple and who must establish legal parentage through an adoption proceeding. Terms that are equivalent to second-parent adoption include co-parent adoption and confirmatory adoption.

is a genetic father and may be recognized as the legal parent either through a surrogacy parentage order, or an acknowledgement of paternity. The nongenetic father does not become a legal parent through the marital presumption. He must establish legal parentage by way of a court judgment in a surrogacy proceeding establishing his legal parentage, or a confirmatory adoption. This couple will most likely obtain a prebirth order of legal parentage that will name both as the legal fathers. However, depending on the laws and legal process of the state where the birth order of parentage is obtained, the couple may still be advised to do a confirmatory adoption to confirm and secure the legal parentage of the nongenetic father.

On a case-by-case basis, there may be exceptions to this standard advice to do a confirmatory adoption. For example, in Connecticut, the intended fathers to a gestational surrogacy arrangement will obtain a court judgment of legal parentage. As a result of Connecticut's Supreme Court case of *Raftopol v. Ramey*,[44] establishing legal parentage by being a party to a valid gestational agreement is analogous and equivalent to establishing parentage through adoption. Therefore, when legal parentage is accomplished by a Connecticut prebirth judgment, the confirmatory adoption is unnecessary.

It is important to note that being named on a birth certificate does not convey or establish parental rights. It merely creates a presumption of legal parentage. For the lesbian couple, this marital presumption of parentage is not legally safe due to ongoing political and social efforts to dismantle and overturn marriage equality. For example, recently US Supreme Court justices Alito and Thomas made known their opposition to *Obergefell v. Hodges* (the US Supreme Court case ruling in favor of marriage equality), offering an opinion that employees of the government should be able to refuse services to gay married couples if providing services would interfere with their religious beliefs.

In another recent example of efforts to discriminate, the state of Indiana, in the case of *Box v. Henderson*, attempted to deny same-sex couples the same presumption of parenthood that is afforded to opposite-sex couples. However, as Yale Law School professor Douglas NeJaime and GLAD attorney Patience Crozier wrote in the *Connecticut Post*:[45]

> [T]he U.S. Supreme Court once again affirmed that states have an obligation to provide all children equal access to the security of legal parentage regardless of the gender of their parents. This is a tremendous relief, but also a reminder that Connecticut must act so that our laws are clear and inclusive regardless of what happens at the court. By passing the Con-

44. 12 A.3d 783 (2011); 299 Conn. 681 (2011); and see *Raftopol v. Ramey* in Court Listener (Free Law Project), https://www.courtlistener.com/opinion/2555256/raftopol-v-ramey/.

45. Douglas NeJaime, and Patience Crozier, "Opinion: Conn. Can Take a Stand for Equality," Connecticut Post, December 26, 2020, retrieved April 10, 2021, https://www.ctpost.com/opinion/article/Opinion-Conn-can-take-a-stand-for-equality-15826882.php.

necticut Parentage Act, Connecticut would continue to lead on LGBTQ equality.

Indiana, like every state, maintains a marital presumption of parentage. When a married woman gives birth, the law treats a male spouse as the legal father, whether he is the biological father. Two years after its landmark marriage equality ruling in *Obergefell v. Hodges*, the Supreme Court held in *Pavan v. Smith* that Arkansas must identify a birth mother's female spouse as a parent on the child's birth certificate, just as it does for a male spouse. Consistent with this precedent, the Seventh Circuit Court of Appeals in *Box v. Henderson* held that Indiana's refusal to apply its marital presumption to same-sex couples violates the Constitution.

Yet the Indiana Attorney General incorrectly insisted that the state's marital presumption statute requires a genetic connection between parent and child and asked our country's highest court to exclude same-sex couples from the invaluable protections that legal parentage provides. The marital presumption ensures, at birth, that children born to a married couple are the legal children of both spouses, entitled to the benefits that legal status affords, including custody, decision making, health insurance and inheritance rights. Indiana sought to make LGBTQ parents legal strangers to their children and to force these parents to undergo a time-consuming, expensive, and invasive process of adoption to secure legal parentage.

Pavan, Obergefell and now the court's denial of Indiana's petition in *Box* make clear that the Constitution requires states to treat same-sex and different-sex couples equally. This includes treating nonbiological mothers in married same-sex couples as legal parents, just as the state treats nonbiological fathers in married heterosexual couples as legal parents.

Because efforts to discriminate are ongoing and marriage equality, although settled US Supreme Court law, remains a target to be overruled, same-sex couples are unable to completely rely on the marital presumption of legal parentage. The couple should obtain legal advice and seriously consider legal procedures for the nongenetic parent to become a legal parent through an adoption decree. This will create certainty in terms of the legal parentage of the nongenetic parent. It will also establish stability and security for the child and his or her parents and the legal security and stability of their family.

What Is Reciprocal Reproduction?

"Reciprocal IVF is an option for lesbian couples and trans men who have functional female reproductive organs to participate in the actual IVF and gestation process. Reciprocal IVF is also commonly referred to as partner IVF, partner-assisted reproduction, reception of oocytes from partner (ROPA), or comaternity IVF."[46] Another term to describe this is simply comaternity.

---

46. Resolve (The National Infertility Association), "Reciprocal IVF," (n.d.), retrieved April 10, 2021, https://resolve.org/what-are-my-options/lgbtq-family-building-options/reciprocal-ivf/.

One woman or partner contributes her eggs. She goes through ovarian stimulation to produce multiple eggs. These are retrieved from her ovaries by clinical egg retrieval done at a fertility clinic. The eggs are then fertilized with the sperm of a sperm donor through IVF (in vitro fertilization). The embryos are thus created, at which time the other woman (spouse or partner of the egg contributor) undergoes an embryo transfer by the fertility physician. She then hopefully becomes pregnant with the embryo created from the egg of her spouse/partner and the donor sperm. This is a way that both women can biologically participate in the process to bring their baby into the world.

Although this family formation method is not a gestational surrogacy arrangement, it is worthwhile describing since some people engaging in this process do ask if the pregnant partner can be deemed a surrogate. They ask this to see if they can use surrogacy legal proceedings to establish parentage through a prebirth or post-birth order in accordance with surrogacy laws. But this is neither possible nor desirable. A gestational surrogate is not an intended parent, whereas the intended parent who is the birth parent carrying an embryo to which she is not genetically related, by definition, is an intended parent and, therefore, not a gestational surrogate.

Legal Concerns of Reciprocal Reproduction

In these comaternity arrangements, the woman who is not the birth mother must adopt the baby even though she is the one who is the genetic (egg contributor) mother—that is, the contributor of the egg to the creation of the embryo. If the couple is married, the nonbirth mother's name may go on the birth certificate by way of the martial presumption but, as discussed above, this is not enough to fully secure legal parentage. This may seem strange, but since the genetic mother has not given birth to the baby, her name on the birth certificate creates only a presumption of legal parentage and she should proceed to fully establish her parental rights through the confirmatory adoption.

The biological/birth mother becomes the legal mother by virtue of the fact of giving birth to the baby. This fact that she is the birth mother, even if she is carrying a baby not genetically related to her, establishes her status as legal parent. However, she and her spouse must take steps to confirm and secure the legal parental status of the nonbirth mother through second-parent adoption.

Further, this couple must also be aware that the standard informed consent forms at the medical clinic may not accurately describe that their intentions are to be co-parents. It is very possible that the IVF clinic will provide this couple with consent forms that are not appropriate for them in that they do not cover what is happening. Some clinics may inaccurately refer to the contributor of the egg as an egg donor, but this would be legally flawed for this couple because the egg contributor should not be categorized as an egg donor. An egg donor will not have legal rights to the baby. At the clinic, when signing informed consent documents, the birth mother may sign forms stating that she is the recipient parent, which is also not appropriate because the word *recipient* in assisted reproduction means the person who is the intended parent receiving gametes from a donor who will not obtain legal parental rights.

Therefore, the couple planning comaternity or reciprocal reproduction is advised to consult with legal counsel, who should review the consent forms to be signed at the clinic. Legal counsel should modify these forms, if necessary, to fit the circumstances of the comaternity and the plan for both women/partners to become legal parents.

14

Reproductive Medicine and Gestational Surrogacy

Medical Procedures

The assisted reproduction medical procedures for gestational surrogacy are complicated and must be conducted with the advice and management of a competent reproductive endocrinologist (fertility specialist). Medical technology has evolved and continues to advance rapidly in the field of reproductive medicine, and there are many good and safe medical options and procedures for people to pursue when planning gestational surrogacy.

The first step is to find the reproductive physician and fertility clinic with knowledge and experience assisting patients through the gestational surrogacy process. The physician will discuss the medical options with the intended parents and, together, plan to create the intended parents' embryos and move toward achieving a pregnancy with a surrogate.

Medical Testing/Screening of the Intended Parents

The next step will be for the physician to do testing and screening. There will be a semen analysis of the intended father's sperm or, if a gay couple, both intended fathers' sperm. If the couple is heterosexual, and they are planning to use the intended mother's eggs, there will also be tests to determine if her egg reserve and hormone levels are sufficient to create embryos through IVF (in vitro fertilization).

Semen analysis (sperm count test), analyzes the health and viability of a man's sperm. Semen is the fluid containing sperm that's released during ejaculation. A semen analysis measures three major factors of sperm health:

- the number of sperm
- the shape of the sperm
- the movement of the sperm, also known as "sperm motility."[47]

---

47. Shannon Johnson, "Semen Analysis and Test Results," medically reviewed by Alana Biggers, MD, Healthline, July 13, 2017, https://www.healthline.com/health/semen-analysis#TOC_TITLE_HDR_1.

To get the analysis done, the intended father(s) will ejaculate into a cup at the medical clinic, and the samples will then be tested and analyzed. The results of the semen analysis will give the physician important information and insight into whether or not the man will be able to use his sperm for the embryo creation, or if there are any problems, what the probability of creating an embryo will be, as a percentage.

If the intended parents are a straight couple, and the intended mother is planning to try to use her own eggs, then she will undergo testing as well. There are several tests used to determine if she can effectively use her eggs to make embryos. These tests include the following:[48]

The AMH test: Each egg in a woman's ovaries lives inside a follicle, a fluid-filled sac that contains cells that support egg maturation and produces hormones. AMH is one of those hormones. The level of AMH in a woman's blood helps doctors estimate the number of follicles in her ovaries; the more follicles a woman has, the more eggs she can release, and the better her chances of pregnancy.

The FSH test: Another routine test looks at FSH (follicle-stimulating hormone), a hormone released by the pituitary gland in the brain. FSH drives the growth of ovarian follicles, which, in turn, produce hormones including AMH, estrogen and progesterone. FSH supports ovulation and helps the ovaries mature eggs for each cycle. A woman's FSH levels fluctuate daily throughout her monthly menstrual cycle, spiking immediately before ovulation. But if her levels are generally above or below what is expected for her age, that often indicates one of several problems that might end up affecting not only her fertility but also the chances that IVF will be successful. For example, very low levels may mean a woman has irregular cycles, which can make getting pregnant difficult. High levels may signal that a woman's body is making up for a diminished ovarian reserve by producing more FSH to stimulate ovarian function. Understanding FSH levels and what they mean is complicated, but the information can help doctors decide on treatment options.

There are other tests for infertility, such as a pap smear to check for cervical cancer, or a hysterosalpingogram to determine if a woman's uterus and fallopian tubes are working properly. The physician treating and assisting the intended parents on their journey to have children through assisted reproduction and surrogacy will advise and recommend tests and procedures to optimize the possibilities for a successful outcome.

Creating Embryos

The term *embryo* refers to the development of the group of cells after the sperm fertilizes the egg in reproduction. Each embryo begins development

---

48. Carrie MacMillan, "Women, How Good Are Your Eggs?" Yale Medicine, August 2, 2018, https://www.yalemedicine.org/news/fertility-test.

as a zygote.[49] The zygote divides into more cells, and this collection of cells is called the blastocyst. Technically, the fertilized egg is deemed an embryo from the fifth to the tenth week of pregnancy. However, this term, *embryo*, is generally used to describe the fertilized cell collections that are growing in the IVF clinic laboratory after fertilization.

The term *blastocyst* refers to the day five and day six ball of cells that has developed after fertilization. Blastocysts are important because "[a]n embryo that has reached the blastocyst stage . . . of development has a good chance of making a baby. . . .We know that the embryo is still growing and is a good choice for transfer to the uterus."[50]

The creation of the intended parents' embryos is a critical step in the gestational surrogacy process. Once the initial testing and analysis of the sperm and egg quality are done, the intended parents will decide, with the help and advice of their reproductive physician, how the embryos will be created—that is, whose egg and sperm will be used to create the embryos. In some cases, it will be the sperm of the intended father, or if a gay male couple, the sperm of both intended fathers, and in some cases, it will be donor sperm. Similarly, in some cases, the eggs of the intended mother will be used, and in some cases, donor eggs will be used.

Using the Intended Parents' Eggs and Sperm

Some couples will try to use their own eggs and sperm. The intended father will deposit his semen sample at the medical clinic, and this will be frozen and stored for use to fertilize the eggs at the time of the egg retrieval from the intended mother. Usually, the process that the intended mother will undergo is that she will use injectable medications to stimulate her egg production. She will be closely monitored to see how the follicles with the eggs are developing and how many follicles she has. Once the eggs are ready to burst out of the ovary, the physician will perform a procedure called an egg retrieval and the eggs will be taken from the ovaries.

The retrieved eggs will then be fertilized by way of in vitro fertilization. As stated, the resulting embryos will develop for several days, preferably five or six, to reach the blastocyst stage, and then they will be cryopreserved to await the embryo transfer into the uterus of the gestational surrogate.

Using an Egg Donor

Some couples and some single intended parents will need to use an egg donor to create their embryos. The process for creating embryos will be similar except that the eggs will be retrieved from the ovaries of the egg donor

---

49. *Britannica*, "Zygote": Fertilized egg cell that results from the union of a female gamete (egg, or ovum) with a male gamete (sperm). In the embryonic development of humans and other animals, the zygote stage is brief and is followed by cleavage, when the single cell becomes subdivided into smaller cells," https://www.britannica.com/science/zygote.

50. Fertility Answers, https://www.fertilityanswers.com/everything-you-ever-wanted-to-know-about-embryos-but-were-afraid-to-ask/

instead of from the intended mother. The need for an egg donor will be applicable to a gay male couple, to a single intended father, to a straight couple if the intended mother cannot use her eggs due to age or illness, and to a single intended mother who cannot use her eggs, again due to age or illness.

In these cases, the intended parents must search for and select an egg donor. They may be able to find an egg donor through their fertility clinic. Many clinics have egg donor programs in their clinical services. If the intended parents do not find the egg donor at the clinic, there are egg donation agencies where they can continue their search for an egg donor. Whether it is within the fertility clinic's program or an outside egg donation agency, the intended parents will access the program's database of egg donor profiles, and here they will learn a great deal about prospective donors. When they find a donor they like, they will ask the program coordinator if and when that egg donor will be available to go through an egg donation cycle to donate her eggs to the intended parents.

Using a Sperm Donor

Male fertility is a factor for some intended parents who turn to gestational surrogacy. They will need a sperm donor. Also, lesbian couples and single intended mothers and some transgender intended parents will need a sperm donor.

Finding and accessing a sperm donor is simpler than finding and using donor eggs. The retrieval/donation process for the sperm donor is nothing like the medically invasive nature of egg donation. There are known and unknown sperm donors and laws that relate to sperm donation. There are cryobanks where the sperm of screened and vetted donors may be obtained. Some may be able to find donors who are friends or relatives.

Intended parents seeking a donor through social media and who are not using a standard cryobank must be careful about whom they choose. For an extreme example, look at the case of the sperm donor, Ari Nagel. New York college professor Ari Nagel is the biological sperm donor for more than eighty children. Some national tabloids dubbed him "the sperminator." He told Fox News that, as of May 4, 2021, he had "15 women currently pregnant in AL, CT, FL, MD, NY, NJ, TN and TX plus one in Europe" and that he had eighty-four children.[51]

Using Both Egg and Sperm Donors

Some single parents and couples may need to use a sperm donor and an egg donor. There are heterosexual couples for whom an egg donor is necessary due to the health or age of the intended mother. At times, these couples choose to use a sperm donor as well to balance the gamete contribution, in which case, neither parent will have a genetic connection to the child. This is an approach that obviously not all couples will need to explore, but it works for some couples.

---

51. Courtney Moore, '*Sperminator* who's close to fathering 100 children says 'don't focus on me,' https://www.foxnews.com/lifestyle/sperminator-close-fathering-100-children-speak-dr-oz.

P and C are a couple who used both donor eggs and donor sperm. They needed to use an egg donor due to P's age and they planned to also use a sperm donor to make embryos that would have no genetic connection to either of them.

C was over fifty years old. His first marriage ended in divorce. After the divorce, he met P and they married. They had a dream of having a child together and, after they were together for three years, they embarked on their plan to have a baby through gamete donation and gestational surrogacy. C said that having a family with P would fulfill their dreams. P said that she always dreamed of having a baby. She said that she and C liked to live their lives together including watching a movie or going out with friends and family, and they wanted to share their joy with a child. P and C's baby was born in 2019.

Gestational surrogacy for HIV+ Intended Parents

Intended parents who are HIV+ can turn to gestational surrogacy to have children. Serodiscordant couples, where one partner is HIV+, and seroconcordant couples, where both partners are HIV+, will most likely have the option to be matched with a gestational surrogate. They can have their sperm samples washed and engage in IVF and surrogacy and have children. There are well-known sperm-washing methods that can remove any trace of HIV from the semen. The sperm itself is not fluid, so it does not have HIV associated with it. The sperm is separated from the fluid by the washing process so that it is safe to use the sperm in IVF to create embryos and to safely transfer these embryos to the uterus of the gestational carrier.

> The Special Program of Assisted Reproduction (SPAR) is an international program designed to protect wives, surrogates, and babies from becoming infected during fertility procedures that use sperm from men who desire to have children genetically related to them, but are living with a sexually transmitted disease, such as HIV. The program is based on research findings that some, but not all, of the semen specimens produced by men infected with HIV, hepatitis B and C, and cytomegalovirus (CMV) will test positive for the infectious agent. SPAR scientists, headed up by Dr. Ann Kiessling, are pioneers in assisted reproductive technologies, and have been developing reliable semen testing procedures for twenty-five years. The laboratory methods are licensed by the Massachusetts Department of Public Health, certified by the US government (CLIA) and registered with the US Food and Drug Administration.[52]

In 1999, the first baby was born in the United States to a serodiscordant couple. Thereafter, "[i]n 2002, the American College of Obstetricians and Gynecologists and the American Society for Reproductive Medicine recommended sperm washing for IVF to serodiscordant couples as a standard of

---

52. Bedford Research Foundation Clinical Laboratory, Special Program of Assisted Reproduction, https://www.bedfordspar.org/.

care. Next, in 2006, the HIV Assisted Reproductive Technologies (HART) program saw the light. It had 100% success with all mothers, surrogates, and babies testing negative for HIV."[53]

For intended parents interested in such medical procedures and evaluation, the first step is to be examined regarding duration of the HIV infection and current health status. Semen specimens will then be collected to be analyzed for viral load. The intended parent can collect his semen specimen in the privacy of his own home and have it shipped to the clinic or lab where the analysis and sperm-washing procedures will be done.

---

53. Alex Sunshine, "What Sperm Washing Process Is and How It Helps HIV-Positive," *IVF and Egg Donation Blog*, Sunshine, February 11, 2019, https://www.eggdonors.asia/blog/sperm-washing-process-hiv-ivf/.

Insurance Matters

The Need for Insurance Professionals

One of the major matters in surrogacy arrangements is insurance. There are several insurances that intended parents and surrogates must consider and put in place to be financially protected throughout the journey. The need for reputable and knowledgeable insurance resources and a team of insurance professionals is critical.

Many intended parents seek information from insurance brokerages that specialize in insurance products for matters involving assisted reproduction, such as surrogacy and egg donation. Products that are offered may include surrogacy maternity insurance, life and/or disability insurance for surrogates, egg donation complications insurance, and newborn medical insurance. There are other insurance options that intended parents will learn about during their consultations with these insurance experts.

Other insurance services include medical insurance policy validation (a review of the maternity policy to check if it will cover a surrogate pregnancy), claims management (submission of medical bills to the insurance carriers), and services that include medical bill negotiation when insurance is not available.

It is important for intended parents to set up consultations with such an insurance broker to learn what they need to obtain, how to obtain these insurances, and how much they will cost.

Maternity Options: Medical Insurance for Surrogate Pregnancies

ACA

"The Affordable Care Act (ACA), formally known as the Patient Protection and Affordable Care Act, and colloquially known as Obamacare, is a landmark US federal statute enacted by the 111th United States Congress and signed into law by President Barack Obama on March 23, 2010. Together with the Health Care and Education Reconciliation Act of 2010 amendment, it represents the US healthcare system's most significant regulatory overhaul and expansion of coverage since the enactment of Medicare and Medicaid in 1965."[54]

One of the major provisions of the ACA is that the health insurance policies issued under this law must include coverage for maternity. For this reason, the ACA has become a popular insurance vehicle to obtain medical insurance for surrogates. Still, not all ACA policies will cover surrogate maternity, so this option must be scrutinized by insurance professionals to make sure that if a health insurance policy is procured for a surrogate under the ACA, the policy does not have a provision excluding coverage for surrogate pregnancies.

Lloyd's of London Primary Surrogacy Maternity Insurance

If the surrogate's insurance is in question, one possibility is to obtain surrogacy maternity insurance policies underwritten by Lloyd's of London. These policies require a premium and further funding of a very high retention amount (deductible) that may range from $15,000 to $40,000 or more, depending on the level of the plan, single or twin pregnancy, and other factors.

The benefit of the Lloyd's policy is that it is strictly for a surrogate pregnancy, so there is no chance of a loophole being used to deny coverage. The downside is the cost. For the most part, these policies amount to something like self-pay plans. The funds representing the retention amount (deductible) are used pay medical bills. If the deductible is not fully used, funds are returned to the intended parents. If the funds are fully used, the policy of insurance kicks in to cover the unpaid bills.

Lloyd's Backup (Contingency) Surrogacy Maternity Insurance

Another option is to obtain the Lloyd's of London backup or contingency plan of insurance. For this, the intended parents will make a nonrefundable deposit of approximately $3,000 toward the premium. This gives the parents the option to access the insurance in the event of high medical bills coupled with a denial of claims made to the surrogate's underlying medical insurance. If the policy must be utilized, these policies require a premium in addition to the initial deposit and further funding of a very high retention amount, as stated above.

Again, the retention amount is used to pay the medical bills until it is exhausted. After that, the insurance would pay the medical bills. If there is an insurance denial and the pregnancy and birth are routine without complications, it is most likely that the intended parents will not activate this back-up policy. They will negotiate with the hospital and medical providers, self-pay the medical bills, and not elect to pay the premiums and retention amount for the insurance. However, the option to pay for and activate this insurance would be very important in the event of medical complications and high medical bills.

---

54. *Wikipedia*, "Affordable Care Act," https://en.wikipedia.org/wiki/Affordable_Care_Act.

Life Insurance for Surrogates

Death is a risk of pregnancy, labor, and delivery. It is not common, but there have been times when a surrogate has died in childbirth. This is the most serious risk of becoming a surrogate and, for this reason, it is expected that the intended parents will pay for a life insurance policy for the surrogate.

There are different kinds of life insurance. Whole life insurance policies are investment vehicles where a person takes out a policy and pays a large premium each year, and this is a way of saving and investing money so that the policy gains value and the insured person can access money as he or she would from a savings account. This is not the kind of life insurance that intended parents would get for a surrogate.

Instead, intended parents would pay for a term life insurance policy, which would have a premium that is much more reasonable. The premiums are connected to the amount of life insurance, also known as the death benefit. The usual practice is to obtain policies with a death benefit of around $500,000 to $750,000. The premiums for a term policy for these amounts of a death benefit will be reasonable. There is also an option for intended parents to get life insurance which provides the necessary benefit for the surrogate and includes a benefit to be paid to the intended parents.

Newborn Insurance

Intended parents must arrange for insurance for their newborn baby. This is separate insurance from the maternity insurance that covers the medical treatment for the surrogate. The baby is not eligible for health insurance coverage through the surrogate's health insurance because the baby is not legally the surrogate's dependent baby.

Most intended parents who live in the United States have medical insurance for themselves, and they plan to add their baby to their existing health insurance policies. The important thing in these circumstances is for the intended parents to check with their insurance carrier that they may add their baby as a dependent on their policy. They must check the procedures for adding the baby. There may be time frames or deadlines for the intended parents to notify the insurance carrier that they are expecting a baby. Further, the intended parents must make sure that the baby will be covered even if the baby is born in a different state from where the intended parents live or work.

For international parents, newborn medical insurance is a difficult issue because most of them do not have private medical insurance that will cover them or their newborn baby in the United States. They must address the issue of newborn insurance and find a way to obtain it.

Some parents want to try to have twins. There are serious risks associated with a twin pregnancy. First and foremost are the medical risks and danger for the babies and the gestational surrogate. This type of pregnancy would be deemed high-risk and not recommended by fertility physicians.

For international intended parents, an additional major concern is the financial risk. Almost all women carrying a multiple pregnancy (two or more fetuses) give birth earlier than their due date. While many of the babies ultimately do well, they may most likely spend a week or more in the hospital's neonatal intensive care unit. These medical bills may be $10,000 or more per day per baby. Medical bills for premature infants will skyrocket in no time, and, without medical insurance, this may be financially disastrous.

Even for a singleton pregnancy, it is imperative that the intended parents procure medical insurance for their baby. The insurance for a single baby is more affordable through various programs. Some intended parents may ask if the surrogate's medical insurance will cover the baby. Some insurance policies have a provision that the newborn will be covered under the birth mother's policy for up to thirty days. The intention of these provisions is that the insurance will cover a newborn who is a legal dependent of the birth mother. However, the newborn in surrogacy arrangements is not the legal child or dependent of the surrogate.

Some might also ask that if the intended parents obtain a post-birth order of legal parentage, then, at the time of the birth, the surrogate may still be deemed the legal mother and, therefore, it is arguably acceptable to use the surrogate's insurance for the newborn. This is not legally sound because the gestational surrogacy agreement states that the surrogate is not the legal mother of the baby and has no intention of becoming the legal mother. Further, the intended parents are claiming in the agreement that they are the legal parents and that they are responsible for the parental obligations related to the baby. Therefore, trying to use the surrogate's insurance for the baby is not legal and may even be found to be insurance fraud.

Egg Donation Complications Insurance

This type of insurance is procured in every case where an egg donor is used to create embryos. The recipient parents will be responsible for the routine costs related to the egg donation such as medication, medical procedures for examining and monitoring the egg donor, and the egg retrieval clinical procedure. There are potential medical complications and risks to the egg donor. In the event she sustains medical complications, egg donation complications insurance covers those medical expenses.

Other Surrogacy-Related Insurances and Billing Management Assistance

Loss of Reproductive Organs Coverage

In almost every gestational surrogacy agreement, there is a provision for a payment to the surrogate if she loses her reproductive organs either partially or totally because of the surrogate pregnancy or medical treatment directly related to becoming a surrogate. These payments may range from $4,000 to $6,000 for partial loss of reproductive organs and $6,000 to $10,000 for the full loss of reproductive organs.

A woman's reproductive organs include her uterus, cervix, two fallopian tubes, and two ovaries. So, for example, the loss of one fallopian tube due to an ectopic pregnancy will trigger the payment to the surrogate for the partial loss of reproductive organs.

It is possible to obtain an insurance policy that will cover this payment in the event there is such a loss. The intended parents may choose to add this type of insurance to their list of insurances so that this payment will be made on their behalf by the insurance company.

Income Replacement: Short- and Long-Term Disability Options

Another aspect of the gestational surrogacy agreement is the need to reimburse the surrogate for lost wages for specific circumstances related to the surrogacy journey. There is sometimes a cap or limit on lost wages, and this may range from $5,000 to $20,000. Some surrogacy agreements may not have a limit on lost wages. With this omission, it is necessary to clearly define and specify when and for what reasons the surrogate may claim lost wages.

If the gestational surrogate is employed, the agreement will state that she is to be reimbursed for time off from work that is directly related to the surrogacy process. She will be reimbursed for trips to the clinic for the physical examination and the embryo transfer trips, and she will be reimbursed for the days she is in the hospital for the birth as well as for her recuperation after the birth, usually from six to eight weeks.

Another reason that the surrogate may need reimbursement for lost wages is if she is placed on bed rest during the pregnancy by her treating physician. "Bed rest in pregnancy—more accurately called 'activity restriction,' can mean anything from cutting back on your work hours to staying in bed most of the time."[55] Some reasons a surrogate might be ordered by the doctor to be on bed rest include:

- a risk of preterm labor [if the pregnancy is a twin or multiple pregnancy]
- intrauterine growth restriction (the baby isn't growing properly)
- placenta previa (a placenta that lies unusually low in the uterus, covering the cervix)
- gestational hypertension or preeclampsia (to keep blood pressure in check)
a history of miscarriage.[56]

Outsourcing Medical Billing Management

As with all medical treatment for which there is health insurance, surrogacy is an area that requires oversight and management related to insurance claims

---

55. Karen Miles, "Bed Rest During Pregnancy," medically reviewed by Sally Urang, MS, RN, SNM, midwife, Babycenter, May 20, 2021, https://www.babycenter.com/pregnancy/health-and-safety/bedrest-does-it-help_208#articlesection2.

56. Karen Miles, "Bed Rest During Pregnancy," medically reviewed by Sally Urang, MS, RN, CNM, midwife, Babycenter, May 20, 2021, https://www.babycenter.com/pregnancy/health-and-safety/bedrest-does-it-help_208#articlesection2.

management. For some intended parents and surrogates, this may not seem to be an ordeal, and so they may be willing to take this on themselves. However, medical insurance in the United States, in general, is complicated, and in the world of surrogacy, the complications are compounded.

As noted, not all health insurance policies cover surrogate pregnancies. Further, those that do may go through changes or revisions on the renewal dates, which may alter the coverage. The extreme case is when a policy that says it will cover a surrogate pregnancy is modified so that a surrogate pregnancy, previously covered, becomes an exclusion. Someone must be paying attention to these renewal policies. Surrogacy agencies are not insurance brokers and usually put the matters related to insurance in the hands of qualified and competent insurance professionals. This is especially important for international intended parents who are unfamiliar with the health insurance system in the United States.

Outsourcing the medical billing and claims management is a very important and worthwhile consideration. Some surrogacy programs may even mandate this type of management to assist and protect the intended parents and the surrogate. There are services that may be retained to assist with insurance management and the insurance of medical bill claims to the health insurance carrier (the company that has issued the health insurance policy).

The surrogacy agency should have experience with medical insurance policies and may be able to give some advice and guidance on insurance needs and requirements. However, the need for a professional insurance resource is critical to obtain the insurance policy and to review it to ensure it will cover a surrogate pregnancy.

Other services that insurance professionals may offer in the complicated arena of insurance matters include the following:

- providing information about the insurance policy, such as copay amounts, coinsurance, and deductibles;
- submitting medical bills to the insurance company for payment and following up to determine if payment was made;
- handling insurance appeals if there is a denial of a coverage claim;
- Negotiating medical bills if necessary;
- Working cooperatively with surrogacy agencies, fertility medical clinics, and medical treatment providers

PART III

After the Birth

16

Postbirth Questions and Concerns

Birth Certificates

The birth certificate for the newborn baby will be issued shortly after the birth if a prebirth order was done to establish the intended parents or the single intended parent as the parent(s) of the newborn baby. The documentation from the prebirth legal proceedings must be submitted to the hospital where the birth is to take place and to the department of vital records in the state where the birth occurs. The birth certificate is issued from the state office, usually the department of health or department of vital records. The parents will obtain the physical copy of the birth certificate from a county or municipal office in the county or town/city where the birth occurred.

It is worth noting one legal issue about birth certificates—that is, a parent's name on a birth certificate creates a presumption of legal parentage. "A legal presumption is a conclusion based upon a particular set of facts, combined with established laws, logic, or reasoning. It is a rule of law which allows a court to assume a fact is true until it is rebutted by the greater weight (preponderance) of the evidence against it."[57]

The legal presumption that a child born to a woman is the legal child of her spouse is a rebuttable presumption. The presumption may be rebutted by a DNA test proving the spouse is not the genetic father. See Chapter 13, "The Laws of Gestational Surrogacy," for additional discussion on the presumption of legal parentage.

In the following circumstances, the presumption of parentage as shown by the birth certificate is sound and may not be successfully challenged:

1. The named parent has given birth to the child;
2. The named father is a genetic parent and has signed an acknowledgment of legal parentage, or is married to the birth mother;

---

57. USLegal, "Legal Presumption Law and Legal Definition," https://definitions.uslegal.com/l/legal-presumption/#:~:text=A%20legal%20presumption%20is%20a,of%20the%20evidence%20against%20it.

3. The named parent and birth parent execute an acknowledgment of parentage (in a state where the law equates an acknowledgment of parentage with a court adjudication of parentage);
4. The named parent has legally adopted the child; or
5. The named parent has obtained a court judgment of legal parentage in a surrogacy prebirth or postbirth order legal proceeding.

In the following scenarios, the legal presumption of parentage may be challenged, and the named parents should consider following legal advice to do a second-parent adoption:

1. The named parent is a nongenetic parent and is appearing on the birth certificate simply because of the marriage to the birth parent. For example, in the marriage of a female same-sex couple, although their marriage creates a presumption of legal parentage, this presumption can be challenged if the couple breaks up or if the marriage equality law for same-sex couples is weakened or abolished.
2. The named parent is a nongenetic parent and is appearing on the birth certificate because of a prebirth or post-birth order of parentage through a gestational surrogacy arrangement. However, the pre- or post-birth order is not equivalent to an adjudication or court judgment of legal parentage by a court of competent jurisdiction.

Questions remain regarding whether a same-sex couple should obtain legal counsel and do a second-parent adoption to confirm the nongenetic parent's legal parental rights. For example, recently, Connecticut passed the Connecticut Parentage Act, which is based on the Uniform Parentage Act. This law includes a provision that enables a nongenetic parent to enter an acknowledgment of parentage with the birth parent to establish the nongenetic parent's legal parental rights. Will this acknowledgment of parentage (deemed by the law to be equivalent to an adjudication or judgment of parentage from a court of law) be sufficient throughout other US states and other countries as legally recognizable to establish the nongenetic parent's legal parental rights? The answer is that it should be sufficient, but the fact that it should be sufficient is not enough to guarantee that such an acknowledgment will be sufficiently recognized in all other jurisdictions as equivalent to a judgment of legal parentage.

The same concern applies to certain prebirth orders of legal parentage in surrogacy. Another example is the state of Illinois, where the prebirth order is obtained by submitting affidavits and other documentation to the Illinois Department of Public Health. Here, there is no judgment from a court of law, and, therefore, the intended parents should consider completing a confirmatory adoption (a/k/a co-parent or second-parent adoption) to establish the nongenetic parent's legal parental rights fully and finally.

All intended parents going through assisted reproduction, whether married or unmarried, gay or straight, must get legal advice from an attorney experienced and knowledgeable in assisted reproduction technology law to determine the legal documents and legal procedures necessary to protect and secure their families.

International Concerns

International intended parents face concerns and legal issues that must be addressed. Although they can easily become the legal parents of their children in the United States and obtain a birth certificate showing that they are the legal parents of their babies, they must establish themselves as the legal parents of their children in their home countries, and they must establish the citizenship of their babies in their home countries. In most cases this is not automatically achieved. These intended parents must have a home country lawyer to assist them with the legal procedures they must follow to establish their baby's citizenship in their home country and to make sure that the intended parents' parental rights and authority are confirmed and fully established in their home country.

Still, many intended parents come from abroad to the United States to have their babies through gestational surrogacy. There are several very good reasons for this. Although having a child through surrogacy is costly in the United States, the reasons people come here are (1) unmatched legal certainty and security for the enforcement of the surrogacy agreement and the establishment of legal parentage for the intended parents; (2) advanced medical technology for IVF and cryopreservation of gametes and embryos; and (3) a firm ethical framework for gestational surrogacy that focuses on the protection of all parties involved.

Who Will Be Flying Home with Us?

One important and interesting phenomenon that happens at times is the dependence that the intended parents come to have on their agency case managers, lawyers, and other helpful people during their US surrogacy process. Intended parents must realize that many of the details of having a baby will become their responsibility. While the surrogacy agency and the IVF medical clinic, as well as the surrogate and the doctors, provide a great deal of guidance and support throughout the surrogacy journey, the intended parents must prepare for the birth of their baby, as all parents-to-be must do.

One interesting email that came across the desk of a surrogacy agency case manager from a very sweet and lovely international couple read, "Who from the agency will be flying home with us?" This is a good example of the dependence and expectations that may come about from working with a supportive and nurturing surrogacy agency case manager.

If intended parents feel they need support with caring for their new baby, support is available, but this support will come from resources outside the surrogacy agency. For example, some new parents come to the birth of their child with another family member such as a mom, brother, or sister. These supporters most likely have experience with newborns and can assist as the new parents learn how to care for their new baby.

If a family member is not available, intended parents can hire a doula. As dona.org explains:

> The transition into new parenthood can be vulnerable, and postpartum doulas are experts in emotional support, active listening and encouraging new parents to follow their own hearts. Empathy, a hug or even a good laugh together can do so much for a new parent! . . . Postpartum doulas are trained to understand what new babies—and new parents—truly need. The doula helps with soothing techniques, offers lactation or bottle-feeding support, and explains normal newborn behavior and postpartum recovery expectations. . . [P]ostpartum doulas can help the days go by more smoothly by helping with the baby's laundry, doing the dishes, or preparing simple, nourishing meals. . . [P]art of their role is to help the entire family adjust and settle in.[58]

58. DONA International, "Benefits of a Doula," https://www.dona.org/what-is-a-doula/benefits-of-a-doula/.

17

Psychological and Social Issues

How to Talk to Your Children

Intended parents often have questions about how to tell their children about their birth stories. There is no one-size-fits-all on this subject. It is a personal matter for parents, and they must decide what will work best for them within their marriage, family, and social constellation. There are also some important factors to consider, such as the potential for a social stigma regarding surrogacy and assisted reproduction in some countries. Even more significant than a social stigma are actual laws against surrogacy.

In the United States, assisted reproduction is accepted and promoted for intended parents who need such help to have their babies. Yes, there may be discouragingly negative attitudes and misperceptions from some individuals and groups in the United States, but for the most part, it is safe to be open and forthright about utilizing assisted reproduction. There are IVF medical clinics, surrogacy programs, and egg and sperm banks, as well as donor resources; embryo donation banks; social media promoting assisted reproduction; chat rooms for surrogates, intended parents, and professionals; surrogacy insurance resources, and laws and lawyers for intended parents to find legal advice and to establish their legal parentage.

Because of this public attention to assisted reproduction, it is more realistic and likely that intended parents in the United States, as well as in countries where surrogacy is accepted, will tell their children the stories and the facts of how the children were conceived and born.

It is also critical for intended parents to consider their children's potential needs and rights when it comes to knowing about their birth stories. It will likely be a great burden for this kind of disclosure to be made to children when they are older and have already made certain assumptions about their conception and birth only to find that there are important and hidden facts about their origins that were not disclosed to them. Secrets may be harmful, and they have a way of altering family dynamics and relationships that may be damaging. Such important information usually does not remain secret, and parents should assume that their children will find out about their birth stories even if the parents decide not to disclose the information.

Here are some helpful suggestions from VARTA[59] for telling children about their conception and birth stories:

- *There is no "right" or "wrong" way or words to use:* It is not what you say but how you say it that reflects your love and pride in the way you became a family. Hearing this will ensure your child understands they are much wanted.
- *Be confident and proud:* If your child senses that you are embarrassed or ashamed that you used fertility treatment, this may affect the way they feel about themselves. As a result, they may be less likely to want to ask questions or talk to you about it in the future.
- *Don't make it a big deal:* Your child's donor conception or surrogacy story is only one facet of who they are. All children want to feel special but that does not mean they want to feel different from their peers. Try not to refer to your donor or surrogate as if they are a superhero—they are ordinary people who did something extraordinary to help. At the same time, it is important that you convey a high regard for the person who helped you become parents.
- *Remember the first conversation is just that—a beginning:* Your child will have their own thoughts and questions and they need to feel able to talk to you about them. Keep the conversations going—they may need to hear some information more than once. It might also be helpful for them to talk with someone other than you—just as you may benefit from having a supportive friend, family member or counsellor to talk things over with.
- *Every child's reaction is different:* Your child's response may surprise you as they may show little reaction and you may wonder if they have absorbed the information. They may become quiet and need time to process things. Conversely, they may be quite curious. Older children may be shocked or angry; they may also need time and space to deal with what they have learned. They may be sad they do not share a genetic link with you and confused as to what implications this has for their other relationships within the family.

There are also numerous children's books to help parents begin the discussion with their young children about the child's birth story and conception. Here is a partial list:

Grown in Another Garden: A Surrogacy Book for Young Children by Crystal Falk. This book introduces children, ages two to eight, to surrogacy.

---

59. Victorian Assisted Reproductive Treatment Authority (VARTA), "Telling Children, Family and Others," https://www.varta.org.au/after-donor-conception/telling-children-family-and-others.

The Very Kind Koala: A Surrogacy Story for Children by Kimberly Kluger-Bell. This is a picture book for young children that introduces surrogacy through the simple story of a koala bear and her husband who needed the help of a very kind koala to carry their baby in her pouch. Parents can begin reading this story to children as young as three years of age to begin the dialogue about their own helpful surrogate.

The Kangaroo Pouch: A Story about Surrogacy for Young Children by Sarah A. Phillips. This book is geared for the children of surrogates. Oliver, a young kangaroo whose mother becomes a surrogate for the Bouncing-Hopalots and delivers their baby to them, narrates this story, and shows what the gestational surrogacy process is all about from start to finish.

My Mom Is a Surrogate by Abigail Glass. This book was written to help children of surrogates understand the process of the surrogacy journey. It provides the reader with a guide to discuss the surrogacy experience using the proper language through a sweet story and attractive images.

I'm Very Ferris: A Child's Story about In Vitro Fertilization by Tess Kossow. This is an easy-to-read children's book that explains infertility through IVF and celebrates the many ways that families are made. Ferris is a baby boy who has an amazing story about his entrance into the world.

Miracle Baby: How Babies Are Made the IVF Way by Dr. Jennifer Bennett. This book explains IVF to children ages three to seven and is meant for the parent and child to read together.

What Makes a Baby by Cory Silverberg. This book provides a way for children ages three to seven to understand how reproduction works, using scientific terminology (sperm, egg, uterus). The pictures are not gender specific, and the book teaches children that while you need a sperm and an egg to make a baby, not everyone has a baby in the same way, so every family should be able to make use of this book.

The Donor Conception Network has a series of books titled *Our Story* (for ages three to six) that discuss all types of family building, including egg donation.

I Can't Wait to Meet You by Claudia Santorelli-Bates and Caleb Sawyer. This is a story for children ages four to eight. It is about a couple who used IVF to conceive a child. Some technical language is used, so it is probably better for somewhat older children.

How Babies and Families Are Made: There Is More Than One Way! by Patricia Schaffer and Suzanne Corbett. This book for children ages five to nine is a basic sex education book for families formed in alternative ways. It includes a discussion of miscarriage, cesarean delivery, twins, artificial insemination, in vitro fertilization, adoption, and stepchildren. Surrogacy and egg donors are not discussed, but the book is inclusive enough to open the door for this discussion.

Before You Were Born series of books for children by Janice Grimes, RN. These books discuss conception through IVF, egg donation, embryo donation, donor sperm, and surrogacy.

My Beginnings: A Very Special Story by Tim Appleton. This is a story of a mommy and daddy who want a baby. After wanting and waiting, they finally have a baby through IVF. The story can be customized with all the details specific to your story.

Spectacular You: An IVF Love Story by Kate Pache. This is a beautifully illustrated storybook that explains in vitro fertilization to children and the process their parents went through to have them.

Extra! by Kaeleigh MacDonald. This book tells the story of Lucas discovering that it took extra time and patience for his parents to have him. Covering many family-building options, *Extra!* shows that even when parents struggle to conceive, they can go on to become a family, and that being "extra" is wonderful!

Besides buying books, parents can write their own books and stories for their children. The parents know the special details and special people that came along and who were integral people on the journey to the birth of the child. Therefore, parents might consider writing or filming their narratives and stories about having children and use these to talk to their child or children about their conception and birth stories.

Some people have already kept notes, logs, journals, photos, and videos of their surrogacy journeys, and they may want to organize these materials into an album or journal. They may use these materials as resources to show their child or children when they are ready to hear more about their birth stories.

The world of surrogacy is replete with conception and birth stories that involve warm and loving relationships between and among people who come together to bring a newborn baby into the world, with lawyers and doctors who care about helping people to have their children, and with friends and family members who are supportive and loving to the parents and surrogates embarking on and going through surrogacy journeys.

Children are resilient and surprising. They don't carry the same fears and anxieties that adults do about what other people think. I know one small boy who was riding in a car with a friend who had two moms. The little boy said, "Joey has two moms? He is lucky. I only have one mom." This is a true example of how children see things differently, with innocence and openness.

The children born through surrogacy are very wanted and loved children and they will be surrounded by loving parents, grandparents, relatives, and friends. Giving them the information and truth of their conception and birth stories will strengthen them and give them the confidence of knowing who they are.

How to Talk about Your Surrogacy Journey with Family and Friends

This is another very personal topic and there are several parts to it. The first part is when to talk about surrogacy plans with family or friends. The second part is what to say and/or how much to say about your surrogacy plans.

First, remember that this is your story, your journey to parenthood. It is yours to share or not share, and you have control and rights over who gets to know about and share in this personal and wonderful endeavor and milestone in your life. It is like having an adopted child. When my son was young and I took him shopping, people would look at us (he has reddish blonde hair and fair skin, and I have very dark hair and olive skin) and say, "Oh, he must look just like his father." The facts are (1) my son is adopted, and (2) he has two moms. Did I need to explain this to the stranger? No, I did not. There is no need to explain to anyone and everyone the stories of how we build our families.

Second, it really does not make sense to share plans with people who are not supportive. There are some attitudes out there about surrogacy that are negative. In this book and through other organizations, there are very good efforts and successes showing that in the United States, gestational surrogacy is a very positive opportunity for intended parents and surrogates, and the process is conducted within a rigorous ethical framework. But negative attitudes persist, and therefore, parents and surrogates should be selective. Because they have a right to privacy, they are entitled to be selective when deciding with whom they will share their story.

The question of when to tell people will be answered differently by different people. Some people who have gone through serious and difficult infertility may wish to keep the process private until they have a viable pregnancy. This is because it may just be too hard to talk about without intense emotions coming up. Other people who do not have a history of hardship may have an easier time and may be excited to share their plans with relatives and friends. They can decide when it's a good time to tell various people in their lives. Will they share their plans prior to beginning the process? Or will they wait until they have embryos and a surrogate? Or will they wait until they have an ongoing healthy pregnancy.

The objective in making these decisions is to increase happiness and joy; not to increase stress and anxiety. So, if it feels that a discussion with any person or group will be stressful or anxiety provoking, it is perfectly acceptable to wait until it is necessary to disclose facts and circumstances to these individuals or groups.

There are, of course, variations on these ideas and suggestions regarding discussion and disclosure. There may be people with a history of hardship who do want to discuss surrogacy with friends and family, and there may be couples who have no hardship history but who just want to maintain privacy until the time is near for the birth of their baby.

The important thing is that any path is fine if it works for the intended parents. Less stress is better, so if discussing the matter creates stress or anxiety, then privacy is the answer.

18

Estate Planning, Advance Medical Directives, and Powers of Attorney

The term *estate planning* refers to the preparation of tasks that serve to manage an individual's financial situation in the event of their incapacitation or death. The planning includes the bequest of assets to heirs and the settlement of estate taxes . . . Most estate plans are set up with the help of an attorney experienced in estate law.[60]

The most common document in an estate plan is the last will and testament. This document is not only for the purpose of planning for the disposition of assets after death. A will also includes designations of guardians and trustees for minor children. A guardian is the person named to care for and raise children in the event of their parents' death or incapacity. A trustee is the person named who will manage money and assets that the child receives through inheritance. In the will, there will be a trust for minors. This is a set of provisions naming the trustee and describing how the funds may or may not be used for the minor child. Basically, the funds are to be used for health care, education, and other essential needs.

"A living will—also known as an advance directive—is a legal document that specifies the type of medical care that an individual wants in the event they are unable to communicate their wishes."[61]

The point is that people expecting babies and even couples who do not yet have children and who are only in the information-gathering phase of their journey should be thinking about these plans. Couples should have powers of attorney. These are documents by which one spouse or partner gives authority

---

60. Julia Kagan, "What Is Estate Planning? Definition, Meaning, and Key Components," *Investopedia*, April 20, 2021, https://www.investopedia.com/terms/e/estateplanning.asp.

61. The Investopedia Team (reviewed by Ebony Howard), "Living Will: Definition, Purpose, and How to Make One," *Investopedia*, July 14, 2021, https://www.investopedia.com/terms/l/living will.asp.

to the other spouse or partner to do the things they might do for themselves but are incapable of doing. If someone is in a coma or other emergency medical situation, the partner can make decisions for medical care and to take care of financial matters such as banking and paying bills.

Wills, living wills, and powers of attorney are essential estate and life planning documents that individuals and couples should put into place as they are moving through the surrogacy journey toward having children.

Conclusions

Having a child through gestational surrogacy is a complicated process, but when it is managed by a competent team of professionals, it is very safe and secure. Intended parents will become the legal parents of their baby, and they will have a gestational surrogate who is fully committed to providing a healthy pregnancy and to delivering a healthy baby into the arms of the waiting intended parents.

Truly, the only drawback to gestational surrogacy in the United States is the cost. As we have noted, it is expensive, and there are significant bills and expenses to consider. Once the cost is managed, everything else about gestational surrogacy in the United States will fall into place and lead the way to family formation. Once more, we emphasize the need for a competent and experienced professional team, including reproductive physicians, nurses, obstetricians, lawyers, surrogacy and donor agencies, and other surrogacy professionals.

Glossary

Abortion—The termination of a pregnancy after, accompanied by, resulting in, or closely followed by the death of the embryo or fetus. It can be spontaneous or induced.

Alternative reproduction—A process that encompasses in vitro fertilization, sperm donation, ovum donation, and surrogacy.

Altruistic surrogacy (compassionate surrogacy)—A process involving a surrogate, usually a close friend or family member, who offers to carry a pregnancy without a surrogate fee. The intended parent(s) will cover all the incurred expenses that go along with a surrogate agreement, but there is no financial compensation provided to the surrogate.

Amniocentesis—The surgical insertion of a hollow needle through the abdominal wall and into the uterus to obtain amniotic fluid, especially for the determination of fetal sex or chromosomal abnormality.

Assisted reproduction—A general term for medical procedures to assist with achieving a pregnancy including in vitro fertilization and other methods of fertilizing a human egg with human sperm, medical processes involved in egg donation, sperm insemination, embryo transfer procedures, and all medical matters concerning gestational surrogacy.

Assisted reproductive technology law—Law that is comprised of all statutory and case law as well as legal procedures concerning, egg and sperm donation, embryo creation and donation, informed consent for assisted reproduction medical procedures, rights and obligations of gamete donors, gamete recipients, gestational surrogates and intended parents. It includes drafting, negotiation and enforcement of egg and sperm donation agreements, gestational surrogacy agreements, embryo donation agreements and all legal procedures to establish intended parents through surrogacy as the legal parents of their child born through gestational or genetic surrogacy.

Background investigation—A procedure used by an individual or company to verify that individuals are who they claim to be. This provides an opportunity to check and confirm the validity of people's criminal record, education, employment history, and other activities from their past.

Birth certificate—A copy of an official record of a person's date and place of birth and parentage.

Blastocyst—A stage of embryo development that is achieved around five days after the egg is fertilized.

Compassionate surrogacy—See altruistic surrogacy.

Cryobank—A low-temperature facility, storing, for later use, human tissue such as sperm, embryos, cells, and eggs.

CVS (chorionic villus sampling)—The biopsy of a villus of the chorion at usually ten to twelve weeks of gestation to obtain fetal cells for the prenatal diagnosis of chromosomal abnormalities.

D&C (dilation and curettage)—A medical procedure in which the uterine cervix is dilated and a curette is inserted into the uterus to scrape away the endometrium during the diagnosis, or treatment of abnormal bleeding, or for surgical abortion during the early part of the second trimester of pregnancy.

Donor eggs—Eggs that are taken from a fertile woman to be used to create embryos.

Egg bank—A database of frozen donor eggs.

Egg donation—The process by which a woman donates eggs to enable another woman to conceive as part of an assisted reproduction treatment or for biomedical research. For assisted reproduction purposes, egg donation typically involves in vitro fertilization technology, with the eggs being fertilized in the laboratory. More rarely, unfertilized eggs may be frozen and stored for later use. Egg donation is a third-party reproduction as part of assisted reproductive technology.

Egg donation contract—A contract stating that the donor does not intend to parent any child conceived by her egg and does not wish to have physical or legal custody of any eggs harvested during the retrieval process, embryos, or the child or children born as a result of the procedure.

Egg donor—A woman who donates her ova for use in in vitro fertilization.

Egg retrieval—The harvesting of eggs from the ovary that are ultimately destined for artificial insemination and implantation into a recipient uterus as an embryo.

Embryo—The collection of cells in the early stages of fetal growth, from fertilization to the eighth week of pregnancy.

Embryo donation—A procedure that enables embryos that either were created by couples undergoing fertility treatment or created from donor sperm and donor eggs specifically for the purpose of donation to be transferred in order to achieve a pregnancy.

Embryo transfer—The final procedure of the in vitro fertilization process that involves transfer of one or more embryos into the uterine cavity, typically by using a catheter inserted through the uterine cervix.

Escrow account—A legal arrangement in which a third party holds and disperses funds during the surrogacy process.

Escrow management—The payment of funds in accordance with the surrogacy contract.

Fertility clinic (reproductive clinic/IVF clinic)—Specialized medical clinics that assist couples, or sometimes individuals, who want to become parents but for medical reasons have been unable to achieve pregnancy via a natural course.

Fertilization—The process of combining the male gamete, or sperm, with the female gamete, or ovum (egg).

Fetus—A developing human from usually two months after conception to birth.

Gestational carrier (gestational surrogate)—A woman who carries and delivers a child for another couple or person. The eggs used to make the embryos do not come from the carrier.

Gestational carrier contract (surrogacy agreement)—An agreement between intended parents and a gestational carrier and her partner/spouse, if applicable. These contracts can be compensated or uncompensated and are intended to detail the parties' rights, obligations, intentions, and expectations in connection with their arrangement.

Gestational surrogacy—A process involving a gestational carrier who does not have a genetic tie to the child she is carrying. The intended parent(s) undergoes in vitro fertilization (IVF), provides the egg and sperm, and creates an embryo to transfer to the gestational carrier. There are also other circumstances where one of the intended parent(s) will contribute an egg or sperm, but a sperm donor, egg donor, or even donated embryo is used in the process.

Gestational surrogate (gestational carrier)—A woman who carries and delivers a child for another couple or person. The eggs used to make the embryos do not come from the surrogate.

HIV (human immunodeficiency virus)—A virus that attacks cells that help the body fight infection, making a person more vulnerable to other infections and diseases. If left untreated, it can lead to acquired immune deficiency syndrome (AIDS).

Host uterus—The uterus of women who serve as surrogates for intended parents who want their fertilized egg carried to term.

ICSI (intracytoplasmic sperm injection)—A laboratory procedure in which sperm and eggs are retrieved. A single sperm is then injected directly into an egg to fertilize it.

Infertility—An inability to become pregnant after a year of unprotected intercourse.

Insemination—The introduction of semen into a woman by natural or artificial means.

Insurance premium—The amount of money an individual or business pays for an insurance policy. Insurance premiums are paid for policies that cover health care. Failure to pay the premium on the individual or the business may result in the cancelation of the policy.

Insurance deductible—A set amount of money that an insured person must pay out of pocket every year for eligible health-care services before the insurance plan begins to pay any benefits.

Insurance copay—A fixed out-of-pocket amount paid by an insured person for covered services. It is a standard part of many health insurance plans. Insurance providers often charge copays for services such as doctor visits or prescription drugs. Copays are a specified dollar amount rather than a percentage of the bill, and they are usually paid at the time of service.

Intended parent(s)—Individual(s) who enter into an agreement providing that the individual(s) will be the parents of a child born to a surrogate by means of assisted reproduction, regardless of whether either individual has a genetic relationship with the child.

IUI (intrauterine insemination)—An artificial insemination technique in which sperm are put directly into a woman's uterus at the time she is ovulating.

IVF (in vitro fertilization)—An assisted reproductive technique that involves removing sperm and eggs, fertilizing them in a laboratory, and placing a fertilized egg in the uterus.

Legal clearance—Legality evidenced by a letter sent from the attorney to the IVF clinic confirming that the contract has been signed by both the intended parents and the surrogate.

LGBTQ+—Acronym for lesbian, gay, bisexual, transgender, queer or questioning, and others.

Miscarriage—A spontaneous expulsion of a human fetus before it is viable and especially between the twelfth and twenty-eighth weeks of gestation.

Ova—Female gametes (egg cells; plural of *ovum*).

Ovarian reserve—A term that is used to determine the capacity of the ovary to provide egg cells that are capable of fertilization resulting in a healthy and successful pregnancy.

Ovary—An organ found in the female reproductive system that produces an ovum (egg). When released, the ovum travels down the fallopian tube into the uterus, where it may become fertilized by a sperm. There is an ovary on each side of the female body.

Ovulation—The discharge of a mature ovum from the ovary.

Ovum—Female gamete (egg; singular of *ova*). In human physiology, a single cell released from either of the female reproductive organs, the ovaries, which is capable of developing into a new organism when fertilized (united) with a sperm cell.

PGD (preimplantation genetic diagnosis)—A procedure that analyzes biopsied cells from the embryo to identify specific genetic disorders that have a high probability of being passed down from parents to their offspring.

PGS (preimplantation genetic screening)—A procedure that analyzes biopsied cells from the embryo to screen for potential genetic abnormalities when there are no known potentially inherited disorders.

Postbirth order (PBO)—A document establishing parentage submitted to the court by the intended parents' attorney after the baby's birth.

Prebirth order—A document establishing parentage submitted to the court by the intended parents' attorney prior to the baby's birth.

Pregnancy—The period in which a fetus develops inside a woman's uterus, usually lasting about forty weeks.

Psychological screening—A procedure done to determine if a potential surrogate meets the requirements for being a carrier. It involves a standardized objective psychological test and a clinical intake where psychological status, level of functioning, emotional stability, and history are assessed.

Recipient—The individual or couple who receive(s) donated eggs and/or sperm.

Reciprocal reproduction—A process whereby one woman donates her eggs for fertilization and her female partner carries the pregnancy.

Selective reduction—The practice of reducing the number of fetuses in a multiple pregnancy.

Semen analysis—A standard test of a man's semen to check the number and shape of their sperm and its motility.

Seroconcordance—A couple in which both partners are either HIV-positive or HIV-negative.

Serodiscordance—A couple in which one partner has tested positive for HIV and the other has not.

Sperm bank—A facility that purchases, stores, and sells human semen.

Sperm donation—A process in which a man donates semen to help an individual or a couple conceive a baby.

Sperm donation contract—A written legal agreement that defines the rights of everyone involved in a sperm donation arrangement.

Sperm donor—A man who donates his sperm for use in an artificial fertilization process.

Surrogacy agency (surrogacy program)—A service provided by professionals who help coordinate the surrogacy journey for intended parents and surrogates from screening and matching through delivery.

Surrogacy agreement (gestational carrier contract)—An agreement between intended parents and a gestational carrier and her partner/spouse, if applicable. It can be compensated or uncompensated and is intended to detail the parties' rights, obligations, intentions, and expectations in connection with their arrangement.

Surrogacy program—See surrogacy agency.

Surrogate mother—A woman who bears a child on behalf of another person or couple, typically via artificial insemination or in vitro fertilization.

Termination of pregnancy—The medical process of ending a pregnancy.

Traditional surrogacy—The process whereby the surrogate has a genetic tie to the child she carries, which involves being artificially inseminated with the sperm from the male intended parent.

Uterus—The hollow, pear-shaped organ in a woman's pelvis. The uterus is where a fetus (unborn baby) develops and grows, also called a womb.

Resources used for glossary entries:

Grow by WebMD, Glossary of Fertility Terms, https://www.webmd.com/baby/glossary-of-fertility-terms#.

Merriam-Webster, https://www.merriam-webster.com/.

Legal Information Institute (Cornell Law School), https://www.law.cornell.edu/.

American Bar Association (ABA), https://www.americanbar.org/.

Wikipedia, https://en.wikipedia.org/.

Resolve (The National Infertility Association), https://resolve.org/.

Collins, https://www.collinsdictionary.com/.

American Society for Reproductive Medicine (ASRM), https://www.asrm.org/.

ASRM: Reproductive Facts, https://www.reproductivefacts.org/.

American Pregnancy Association, https://americanpregnancy.org/.

New England Fertility Institute, https://www.nefertility.com/

Society for Ethics in Egg Donation and Surrogacy (SEEDS), https://seedsethics.org/.

Investopedia, Dictionary, https://www.investopedia.com/financial-term-dictio-
nary-4769738.

The American Heritage Medical Dictionary, https://medical-dictionary.thefree
dictionary.com/serodiscordant.

Index

About the Author

Victoria Ferrara (Vicki) is an internationally known surrogacy lawyer. She is the Founder & Legal Director of Worldwide Surrogacy Specialists, LLC and she has over 30 years of experience practicing assisted reproductive technology law. She leads with a passion for law and the family formation process to help people make their dreams of family come true—just as hers have. She and her spouse, Michelle Loris, have two sons, Sal, and Nick.

One of Vicki's greatest achievements is the landmark legal decision of *Raftopol v. Ramey*, a Connecticut Supreme Court case that created a new way to establish legal parentage through surrogacy in Connecticut. She has given lectures and presentations at numerous conferences in the United States and throughout the world on gestational surrogacy law and practice, including infertility conferences, gay parenting seminars, medical schools, and other universities, as well as in professional settings for lawyers and physicians. She has published numerous articles and has been quoted in publications including *The New York Times*, *Vice*, *InStyle*, and more.

Vicki was awarded the Lambda Legal Award/Honor and State of CT Proclamation for dedicated and committed career to Equality in 2016, and the Mid-Fairfield AIDS Project President's Award in 2017. She is a member of the Academy of Adoption and Assisted Reproduction Attorneys, the Family Law Institute of the National Gay and Lesbian Bar Association, ASRM, and the American Bar Association Family Law Group.